Quit Smoking Hypnosis: Guided Meditations, Positive Affirmations & Visualizations For Smoking Addiction & Cessation, Replacing With Healthy Habits, Relation & Healing Deep Sleep

by

Self-Healing Mindfulness Academy

© **Copyright 2021 - All rights reserved.**

The content contained within this book may not be reproduced, duplicated or transmitted without direct written permission from the author or the publisher. Under no circumstances will any blame or legal responsibility be held against the publisher, or author, for any damages, reparation, or monetary loss due to the information contained within this book; either directly or indirectly.

Legal Notice:
This book is copyright protected. This book is only for personal use. You cannot amend, distribute, sell, use, quote or paraphrase any part, or the content within this book, without the consent of the author or publisher.

Disclaimer Notice:
Please note the information contained within this document is for educational and entertainment purposes only. All effort has been executed to present accurate, up to date, and reliable, complete information. No warranties of any kind are declared or implied. Readers acknowledge that the author is not engaging in the rendering of legal, financial, medical or professional advice.

This book contains a total of 10 guided meditations, affirmations, and hypnosis scripts to help you quit smoking. The total running time for all the scripts combined will be 10 hours. Proper instructions have been included for the narrator regarding when to pause and resume the narration.

The scripts are in the following order:

I. How this book will make you quit smoking.... 5

II. Quit Smoking Meditations 9

1. Quit smoking visualisation meditation (50 minutes) 9

2. Quit Smoking Contemplation Meditation (60 minutes) 25

3. Quit smoking gradually (70 minutes) 43

III. Quit Smoking Affirmations 67

1. Quit Smoking Affirmations – I (40 minutes) 67

2. Quit Smoking Affirmations – II (60 minutes) 89

IV. Quit Smoking Hypnosis 122

1. Quit Smoking Hypnosis – I (50 minutes) ... 122

2. Quit Smoking Hypnosis – II (60 minutes) .. 140

3. Quit Smoking Hypnosis – III (70 minutes). 156
4. Quit Smoking Hypnosis - IV (70 minutes). 180
5. Quit smoking Hypnosis – V (70 minutes) .. 202

I. How this book will make you quit smoking

Reconditioning the mind

You weren't born with a cigarette in your mouth. You learned to smoke and turned it into a habit. You had to condition your subconscious mind to smoke. And now you crave for cigarettes and find it so hard to quit. But think about it: if you could condition your subconscious mind to smoke, you can recondition it to quit smoking as well. And this is exactly what we are going to do through this book – make you quit smoking by reconditioning your subconscious mind.

Enjoy health and wellbeing

Through this book, you will learn how to get back your control over your life. You will learn to tap into that space within you so that you can experience relief from stress but without cigarettes and at the same time experience even more natural, organic pleasure. You will learn to be in charge of your own feelings and emotions. You will continue to have the good feelings you used to get from smoking and the long-term health benefits of being a non-smoker.

Transform from Slave to Master

Right now, you are on a journey that will transform you from being a slave to cigarettes to being the master of your life. You have had enough of this habit of smoking. It's time to change your life full one eighty degrees. And this would be the first big step on your way to claim your control back.

Feel the benefits of smoking without lighting a cigarette

Through the techniques mentioned in this book you will learn how to nip the cravings in the bud – to stop them right before they start. You will no longer feel the need to smoke cigarettes. Because the relaxation, stress-relief and other good feelings that you used to get from cigarettes, you are now going to enjoy all those feelings without lighting up a cigarette. So, the next time someone offers you a cigarette, you are going to politely refuse the offer by saying, "No, thank you, I don't smoke anymore!"

Find and stick with the technique that works best for you

The content of this book has been designed in such a way that you have enough options to choose from. You may have earlier in life tried to quit smoking but failed. You may have tried many techniques and attended many seminars on how to quit smoking. The reason you are here is that none of them worked for you. So how this book would be any different? How would you benefit from this and finally be able to quit smoking. The beauty of this book is that you have enough options to choose from. What you need to do is try each one of the techniques mentioned in the book. You can try them as many times as you want and then finally stick with the one or two techniques you think are working out for you. By repeatedly practicing any technique you will be able to gain more control over yourself and finally quit smoking forever.

II. Quit Smoking Meditations

1. Quit smoking visualisation meditation (50 minutes)

Congratulations – you are about to say goodbye to cigarettes forever! You have embarked on a journey that will transform you from being a slave to cigarettes to being the master of your life. This meditation is designed make you regain your control over your emotions. You will learn how to nip the cravings in the bud – to stop them right before they start. From this point on, you will no longer feel the need to smoke cigarettes. So let's begin.

Find a quiet spot to meditate. You may choose to sit or lie down as per your comfort. When you are comfortable and ready to begin, gently close your eyes.

Bring your awareness to your breathing. In this meditation, breathing is of upmost importance, so keep a focused attention on your breathing. Breathe in... And breathe out.

[5 seconds pause]

Breathe in... And breathe out.

[5 seconds pause]

Keep breathing with a focus on the flow of your breath.

[20 seconds pause]

Breathing in and out through your nose, feel the breath filling your lungs. Let your ribcage really expand with your breath. In the out breath just let the breath go softly and slowly. Notice how the air feels, coming in and out through your nose. Nice slow deep breath.

[15 seconds pause]

Very good, now slow down your breathing a bit. Be as relaxed as possible.

[10 seconds pause]

Bring your focus into your body, notice how your body feels. Notice any sensations in your body right now. You might feel tingling or pulsing, lightness or heaviness, warmth or coolness or some kind of tightness or you might not feel anything at all, it's completely fine. Notice where you can feel the air as it enters and leaves your body. Whenever you notice your mind wandering, gently bring your mind back to your breath.

[5 seconds pause]

Let your entire body relax, focusing on your body parts one by one. Feel your jaw completely soften and relaxed. The relaxation is meant to take you into a deeper level of trance and healing, so pay attention to the commands. Now imagine breathing right into the base of your stomach, let your belly soften, relax and swell with the in-breath. Very good! Now, on the out-breath let the air go with as little effort as possible.

[5 seconds pause]

Repeat this for the next few breaths, belly swells with the in-breaths and then slowly gently just let the air go. Let the next of your in-breath hold the breath as long as it feels comfortable and natural. Let the exhale become long and smooth.

[5 seconds pause]

Repeat this exercise for the next few breaths. Fill your lungs completely, hold the breath and imagine creating a long smooth thread with your out-breath.

[10 seconds pause]

Feel a calm expansion in your chest area as warm air fills your lungs. Notice this expansion as you hold the breath. Feel your whole body let go and relax with the long smooth out-breath. Be very slow and gentle.

[10 seconds pause]

Notice the way your body respond to these slow, gentle breaths.

[10 seconds pause]

Imagine you can feel in all the muscles in your face. Feel your entire face relaxing and releasing. Be mindful, be relaxed. The relaxation is meant to take you into a deeper level of trance and healing. Now imagine breathing into a forehead, your brow bone, your cheek bone. Feel a sense of relaxation filling deep into your muscles all the way to your skin to your bones. You don't have to force or push tension out, just let go and allow this gentle awareness to naturally release and ease the muscles.

[5 seconds pause]

Feel and imagine all the little muscles around your eyes releasing and relaxing.

[5 seconds pause]

With your lips closed allow your jaws to rest slightly open. Feel all the muscles in your face all smiling.

[5 seconds pause]

Imagine you can breathe all the way into the bones in your scalp. Feel all the muscles in your scalp releasing and relaxing. Be mindful as this relaxation is meant to take you into a deeper level of trance and healing. You might able to feel this happening might feel nothing at all, it's completely fine.

[5 seconds pause]

Imagine layers of tension drifting away from the top of your head; first on the right side of your head, then left side and then back of your head.

[5 seconds pause]

Imagine breathing into the base of your head where spine meets your skull. And feel the sense of relaxation all the way down from your head to your neck, on the right side, then the left side. Feel the sense of relaxation spreading into your upper back. Relaxation is very important. You know how much your body and mind need this relaxation. So whenever your mind wanders away, bring it back to my voice and continue to enjoy this relaxation practice. It's here at top of your spine where different branches of the nervous system meet. Breathe into this point till the top of your neck, the base of your skull.

[5 seconds pause]

Imagine your breath sending a message of calm, spreading down your spine into your torso.

[5 seconds pause]

Feel the sense of calm spreading in from your spine in to all the muscles in your back. And feel it spreading throughout your body, from the tips of your fingers, to the tips of your toes.

[5 seconds pause]

Imagine you can breathe all the way to your back of your lungs in to your shoulder blades and feel the muscles between your shoulder blades gently releasing and relaxing.

[5 seconds pause]

In the next few breaths, imagine that each breath begins at the base of your spine. And as you inhale the breath travels all the way up to the top of your spine. On each exhale the breath gently flows down to your pelvis along your spine back to your tail bone. On each inhale the breath gently flows from the base of your spine all the way to the top of your neck.

[5 seconds pause]

As the breaths turns around and becomes the exhale, dissolve all back down to spine. As your breath gently glides up and down your spine feel your whole body letting go and little more with every breath. May be the breath naturally wants to pose at the top of your spine before you exhale. Or rest in a stillness of the bottom of your breaths before you inhale. Relaxation is very important. You know how much your body and mind need this relaxation. So whenever your mind wanders away, bring it back to my voice and continue to enjoy this relaxation practice. Allow the breath to naturally raise and fall, flow as it chases. Really notice the stillness at the ends of the breath.

[5 seconds pause]

Notice how the out-breath fills gently settling in this stillness and the bottom of the breaths transform and becomes the in-breath, rising above the stillness. Bring your awareness to the movement of your ribcage. Breathe into the sides of your lungs. And feel and sense or imagine all the muscles between your ribs expanding on the in breath and contracting on the out breath. As all the bones in your ribcage swell and release with the breath.

[5 seconds pause]

Allow the sense of relaxation to length of your shoulders and the length of your arms, through your hands.

[5 seconds pause]

Bring your awareness into your legs. Imagine your side bone resting on your hips sockets. Feel the front of your thighs releasing. Feel the back of your thighs relaxing. Feel a wave of relaxation is coming from your hips to your feet.

[2 minutes pause]

See how your body feels lightness, heaviness, sensations or tingling, pulsing. Imagine you can send love to your entire body sending love to your bones, skin everything in between; then to the tips of your fingers to tips of your toes. Notice how your body responds. Invite the deep feeling of peace to gently expand within you and all around you. Feel your whole body immersed in a sense of complete relaxation and calm. Calm and relaxed. Calm and relaxed. Calm and relaxed. Stay in this peaceful feeling for a while.

[5 minutes pause]

Now that you are completely relaxed, let's get to the reason why you are here – to learn how to manage the craving to smoke cigarettes. To beat the craving to smoke, you need to understand how it works. You need to face the craving and manage it. And when you are aware of something and you acknowledge that it is trying to get the better of you, you can put a fight against it. And slowly you will realise that just by acknowledging the craving and its attempt to overpower you, can make the resistance stronger. Then you will no longer be a slave to your craving. You will get your control back. So, what we are going to do today is observing craving to smoke.

[5 seconds pause]

So when you think about a time you craved desperately for a cigarette, how did you feel back then? If you can't think of an incident of desperate craving, think what do you generally feel when you think about smoking a cigarette? Keep that thought running in your mind for a while.

[5 seconds pause]

What's happening in your mind, what's happening in your body? Observe your craving carefully. Now, I want you to think about your craving as a powerful wave in an ocean. The rise and fall of the wave is linked with the intensity of the craving you feel. So at points when the craving is strong, feel the wave rising very high. And when the craving diminishes, the wave also descends.

[10 seconds pause]

Now I want you to start to use your breath like a surf boat. And using this breath like a surf boat, you can ride the wave of craving without getting wiped out. So you are kind of resting your attention on the craving of course by using the breath like it's a surf boat. And you are using the craving as like a wave in the ocean. And just like waves in the ocean cravings rise they get big and then they fall and they go down and they repeat it of down to the shore. When you are breathing, you are using your breath as a surf boat. As you watching each craving come and go, it raises and falls. Perhaps it's a big wave coming up, perhaps it gets really strong. And then it slowly repeats. Perhaps it's a small wave, perhaps there are many waves. Perhaps there are not any of them. Visualise how you are feeling about your craving to smoke.

As if you are on a surf boat, you are using your breath to ride the waves. And as long as you stay with the breath, you stay on your surf boat. So it's really up to you if you want to get over the craving or you want to get wiped out. Allow each wave to rise as high as it wants. Keep your craving in your mind while you visualise the rise and fall of the waves. Focus on the breath to ride the waves.

[5 seconds pause]

Feel how it manifests in the body, in the mind. Perhaps this feels uncomfortable. Perhaps you are finding the exercise easier than you thought it would be. Whatever you are observing, just keep going with the visualisation. Stay with the breath as a surf boat as you rise with each wave of the craving. Feel free to experiment that how much of your attention is on the breath and how much is on the craving.

[5 seconds pause]

Notice the cycle of rising, the crescendo, and how it's subsiding again. Just keep surfing the waves – no matter how big, no matter how small. For the next few minutes, feel free to work with your craving to smoke, a little bit longer.

[5 minutes pause]

If you would like to continue to riding the waves of your craving, feel free to pause this audio and continue your practice for as long as you want to.

[5 seconds pause]

When you are ready, bring your awareness back to the support of your breath. Feel the movement of your breath. Feel the in-breath. Feel the out-breath.

[5 seconds pause]

Feel the in-breath. Feel the out-breath.

[5 seconds pause]

Feel the in-breath. Feel the out-breath.

[5 seconds pause]

Very good, now stay in this feeling of support for a while.

[20 seconds pause]

Now brining your awareness back to the space you are in. Feel where your body touches the bed or the sofa underneath you. Feel your sense of touch.

[5 seconds pause]

Now feel your sense of smell. So you sense any smell? Do not label the smell as good or bad.

[5 seconds pause]

Can you hear anything? What noises can you hear coming from outside the room? Is there any type of noise or disturbance inside the room? Pay attention.

[5 seconds pause]

Now bring your palms together and gently rub them against each other.

[5 seconds pause]

Now place the warmed up palms gently on your eyes and massage.

[5 seconds pause]

Rest your hands in your lap. When you are ready, begin to blink your eyes. Gently open them to come back to the physical world.

[5 seconds pause]

What you have learnt today is one of the most effective ways to manage your craving to smoke. Your breath is always available to be your anchor. Anytime you feel the craving to smoke, just move to the anchor of your breath. Surf on the waves of your breath and the craving will fade away. Continue practicing this mediation for the next few days to master this technique and take your control back over life. Thank you!

2. Quit Smoking Contemplation Meditation (60 minutes)

You are listening to this audio because you have decided to quit smoking. And I believe this decision was made after much thought and introspection. You must have realised that the harmful effects of smoking on your health and life in general far outweigh the good feelings you get from smoking. The good news is that you can be a non-smoker and still continue to enjoy the good feelings naturally. So let get started with today's session. This meditation is one of deep contemplation.

[5 seconds pause]

Sit in a comfortable posture with a straight back. Rest your arms in your lap or place them on your knees. Your comfort is of utmost importance. Feel free to adjust your posture during the course of this meditation. Close your eyes and take an extended breath in and as you do so you will squeeze which ever body part I instruct you through and then on the exhale release that body part as you release that tension, that contraction.

[5 seconds pause]

So begin with the whole right arm, so letting a breath flow through in and out. And now on the next breath in squeeze the hand into a fist and tense the whole right arm, fist, lower arm, upper arm whole right arm squeeze and hold. Exhale let it go.

[5 seconds pause]

Do not think too much if you are doing it the correct way. Just be natural and not too harsh with the contraction and release of the body part. Now move to the left arm as you breathe in squeeze a left hand into a fist and tense the whole left arm, fist, lower arm, upper arm, hold and exhale let it go.

[5 seconds pause]

Very good! Now bring awareness to the whole right leg as you need to breathe and on your next inhale, squeeze the toes, the lower leg, the thigh muscles, whole right leg. And as you exhale release and take a full breath as you take awareness to the left leg. Do not be too hard on your squeezing part. Be natural. The aim is to relax that body part. And on your next inhale, squeeze hold left leg and from the tips of the toes curling in towards the sole, lower leg, thigh everything squeeze and contracted into towards the muscle, or muscle in toward the bone. As you exhale, release. Take a breath in and out.

[5 seconds pause]

Do not be too hard on your squeezing part. Be natural. The aim is to relax that body part. Now will do whole right arm, whole right leg as you breathe in squeeze contract all the muscle in toward the bone, squeeze the toes, squeeze the right fist, whole right side of the body squeeze, exhale and let it go. Do not be too hard on your squeezing part. Be natural. The aim is to relax that body part. So, take a breath. Tune in to the left side of the body. In your own time breathing in squeeze in muscle of the left arm, muscle of the left leg, contract, squeeze, hold, and exhale, let it go.

[5 seconds pause]

We will take one breath in as we prepare it to our full body including the face and the torso as we breathe in squeeze every muscle you can think of and locate in the body including the muscles of the abdomen, face, eyebrows, forehead, nose, mouth everything in towards the centre squeeze, squeeze and hold and exhale. You can let it all go. And simply observe and enjoy your effects of this conscious release.

[5 seconds pause]

Allow the breath to flow freely here there as there is no need to control and direct the breath anymore.

[15 seconds pause]

Then imagine the exhale to be a grounding force for you now. So each time you observe the breath moving through you and out. Imagine that you have settled in just like the closer with earth with the back body.

[5 seconds pause]

Feel as if each continuous exhalation is grounding you.

[10 seconds pause]

Now take notice of anything that becomes more heighten and sharpen to your senses.

[5 seconds pause]

Can you notice anything through the sense of your touch as you feel the temperature of the air can exposed places of the skin?

[5 seconds pause]

Or the touch of clothing against the body?

[5 seconds pause]

Can you notice anything to your sense of taste and from the tongue?

[5 seconds pause]

Sense from nose any sense of aromas coming in through these passage ways of nostrils?

[5 seconds pause]

Now imagine that you can invite these senses inwards or you sense of hearing remains online, taking any external sounds around your in the room or perhaps beyond the walls of the room?

[5 seconds pause]

Bring awareness to your sense of hearing to the sound of my voice. Not necessary to the words I speak but rather allow the sound of my voice to enter through your perception of hearing. If you want to imagine that it's raining right now how would you take in a sound of rain?

[5 seconds pause]

 And in this similar fashion allow my words to follow up on your ears without thought, any analyses. As you draw your sense of hearing closer in now and you take in the sound of any bodily functions and processes; and finally the sound of your own breath.

[5 seconds pause]

You have arrived; welcome yourself here into this space of conscious rest. Remind yourself there is nothing you have to be doing in this moment. Nothing you need to stress for, no desires, outcome, this is actually the place you can let all of that go.

[5 seconds pause]

This practice is a conscious act of non-doing. It's a healing and also exploration of the nominal of these in between spaces in consciousness. So relax. Breathe in. Breathe out. You can welcome yourself here exactly or which means there is no need to compose or mask or costume yourself. And relax. Breathe in. Breathe out. Whatever emotional state you find yourself right now whatever is real for you in this moment. Allow yourself the permission to be exactly that.

[5 seconds pause]

Now give yourself permission to change or shift into a different state throughout today's session. This is a healing game and everything is limitation, everything is optional. Breathe in. Breathe out. While you rest in the faith that your body will receive exactly what it needs today. For what it needs today is to enter a deeper state of meditation that will lead you to quit smoking forever. So relax. Breathe in. Breathe out. As you welcome yourself here, contemplate the part of you who brings you here into this space. This is the part that wants to lead a healthy, smoke-free life. Simply bring that part of you into your awareness. Welcome and thank that part of yourself now.

[5 seconds pause]

Now acknowledge on the land on which you rest, this earth as a whole; the back in direct connect that is supported by the earth below. Imagine what type of earth you could be resting on right now, it could be anywhere in the world.

[5 seconds pause]

Breathe in. Breathe out. Breathe in. Breathe out. Breathe in. Breathe out.

[5 seconds pause]

Bring awareness to your face. Face becomes free from expression. Noticing what is required you to allow yourself to softening through all the muscles in the face. Be relaxed. Breathe in. Breathe out. What is required to experience the softening through the forehead?

[5 seconds pause]

And for the temples – right and left temples to down to the ears? Through the ears down to the earth. And your eyes, both right and left, eyeballs rest back in their sockets.

[5 seconds pause]

Be relaxed. Breathe in. Breathe out. Bring awareness into the jaw, right side of the jaw left side of the jaw and the chin, and the entire jaw releases. Mouth softens.

[5 seconds pause]

Bring awareness to the tip of the tongue. Releasing effort through the tongue and come to the base of the tongue. From the base of the tongue travel down to the throat. You sense the hollowness to the throat. How the throat has the energetic connection to the base of the pelvis. Breathe in. Breathe out.

[5 seconds pause]

Place awareness within the bones of the body. Sense their intensity as they surrender their weight, the muscles around the bones, soften and then the network of inter connected fascia, tissue, fluid. Meditate now on the experience of gravity. Rather than intellectualizing what gravity is, feel experience of gravity.

[15 seconds pause]

Bring awareness into the palm of the right hand. And imagine this gravity to be loving force that just ever so slightly softens the right hand, or fingers, whole right hand.

[5 seconds pause]

Now draw your awareness to right wrist, right elbow joint, right shoulder joint, this gravity comes down softy and hold the whole right arm. And this energy flows down to the right side of torso, the right thigh, the right kneecap, moves down lower leg to meet right ankle joint; softens you through to the top of the right foot, into the sole of the right foot, and all five toes; whole right foot, whole right side of the body.

[5 seconds pause]

Slowing awareness soften you through whole right side. Whole right side surrenders ever slightly closer to earth. The whole right side is relaxed. Breathe in. Breathe out.

Now imagine awareness to land down to the palm of the left hand. This loving force of gravity softens to you through the whole left hand, all four fingers and the thumb.

[5 seconds pause]

You become aware of the left wrist joint. Left elbow joint, left shoulder joint, the whole left arm, the tips of the fingers, the top of the shoulder, relaxed.

[5 seconds pause]

The soft gravitational force cresses the landscape of left side torso. Continue down to the left thigh, rest within the left kneecap.

[5 seconds pause]

Glide down left over leg and softens you through the top of the left foot, into the sole of the left foot. And all five toes.

[5 seconds pause]

Now your whole left foot, whole left side of the body. Whole left side surrenders to the earth. Whole left side is relaxed. Breathe in. Breathe out.

[5 seconds pause]

Bring awareness to the space between the eyebrows. Brow centre and move now on to the space directly behind the surface of the brow centre. And sense its energetic connection down the throat as you land base of the throat.

[5 seconds pause]

This energetic cord continues to descend into the heart centre.

[5 seconds pause]

Down into the navel centre, space just behind the navel point.

[5 seconds pause]

The cord connects all the way down to the base of the pelvic ball.

[5 seconds pause]

As you sense the cord of you now to your inner space.

[5 seconds pause]

The base of the pelvic ball all the way to the space just behind brow centre. From the brow centre space between the eyes.

[5 seconds pause]

Imagine now a silver thread that connects that space directly behind the space of the forehead to the mid brain. Awareness isolates back and forth in rhythm with the breath. Visualizing or imagining a silver thread that connects the space just behind the surface of the forehead, the mid brain. You sense now the right hemisphere of the brain and the left hemisphere of the brain.

[5 seconds pause]

And both hemispheres simultaneously, right and left side all at once. Imagine it grow into the whole body, the whole right side and the whole left side.

[5 seconds pause]

Front side of the body, back side of the body.

[5 seconds pause]

Now from the base of the soles of the feet to the roof, the crown of the head.

[5 seconds pause]

Whole body supported and help as you return to the experience to the earth.

[5 seconds pause]

Now simply observe the breath; observing the breath within the body. Enjoy the experience of the natural cycle of expansion and contraction. Expansion and contraction felt through the breath within the body. As you watch the body breathe in, the earth below rises up to receive the weight of your bones. And you witness this now just inhalations earth rises up to hold you.

[5 seconds pause]

Now imagine that the breath has passively released on the exhalation as the back body is sinking into the earth. Simply witnessing the breath like waves washing up to the shore and reaching back to the ocean. This life energy moves and sinks the breath. This life energy that rides the waves of the breath its right rhythm restores itself. Focus on this energy for a while.

[2 minutes pause]

Coming back now into the mediation. If your mind wandered, don't worry. It's mind's nature to do so. Let's move forward with our meditation, getting ready for the second half now. I want you to visualise yourself in your current situation. Now keeping in mind the ill-effects that smoking has and the pace at which you have been increasing the count of your daily intake of nicotine, I want you imagine that you are now at the end of your life, having smoked your entire life. It's as if you have travelled through time, have smoked all the cigarettes, and have reached the end point of your life.

[5 seconds pause]

Notice how your health is at this point. How would you feel at the end of your life keeping the same lifestyle and the same habits? Think deeply. What regrets do you have having spent your life this way? Do you have any suggestions for your younger self? Take your time. Think freely.

[30 seconds pause]

Now return to the present moment. Keep in mind the lessons you learned. Now take three deep breaths – in through the nose and out through the mouth. In through the nose and out through the mouth. In through the nose and out through the mouth.

[5 seconds pause]

Very good, now relax. Now imagine that you quit smoking today once and for all. And again I want you to travel through time and find yourself at the end of your life. So, you have spent the rest of your life without having smoked a single additional cigarette. You spend your entire life without the harmful effects of nicotine and tar. How do you feel now? How does your health feel? What about the quality of your life? How good do you feel about your life as a non-smoker now? What blessings are you grateful for? And wouldn't you appreciate and thank your younger self for that one life-changing decision to quit smoking? Think about it!

[30 seconds pause]

Now return to the present moment. Keep in mind how you felt this time. Now take three deep breaths – in through the nose and out through the mouth. In through the nose and out through the mouth. In through the nose and out through the mouth.

[5 seconds pause]

You have just travelled across times to witness two alternate lives. Now compare your two future selves. One was full of miseries and regrets and the other full of happiness and gratitude. You are now standing at the crossroads. Now, you know where both the pathways lead to. The choice is yours to make.

3. Quit smoking gradually (70 minutes)

Welcome to this special meditation session to help you quit smoking naturally and effortlessly. Settle into a comfortable position. Gently close your eyes. Start by taking some nice and deep breaths. Release any stress that might be holding in your body. Keep breathing and keep releasing stress.

[20 seconds pause]

Relax and breathe at your natural rhythmic pace.

[5 seconds pause]

We will now be scanning your body from head to toes and toes to head. Throughout this practice you will be guided to move your awareness and attention to the various parts of the body, the sensations and images. There is no need to concentrate to intensely. Simply follow the guidance. If your mind is wanders in between, it's completely fine. Notice this as the natural activity of the mind and then gently with kindness return your attention back to your body. During this practice simply use and observe what you need right now in the moment and leave all the rest behind.

Now take a fully rich inhale. And then release with the intention to let go of anything that no longer serves you.

[5 seconds pause]

Breathing in and breathing out; breathing in and breathing out; becoming aware of the body, releasing tension. Inviting ease, soften; sensing it with the support of the earth beneath you. Feeling fully supported. Feeling the whole body fully supported.

[5 seconds pause]

Feel the feet, supported. Feel the arms and hands supported. Feel the legs supported. Feel the shoulders and head supported. Feel the whole body supported.

[5 seconds pause]

Allow yourself to release into a gentle space of ease. Let go of all stress and tension in the body.

[5 seconds pause]

As you begin to notice the rhythm of the breath, now begin to extend your awareness outward. Listen to the sounds from all directions. Become aware of the distance sounds outside the room.

[5 seconds pause]

Becoming aware of the sounds little bit closer, the sounds inside the room. Becoming aware of the sounds little bit closer yet, sounds of the body. Becoming aware of the sound of your breath; becoming aware of your natural breath.

[5 seconds pause]

Become aware of the natural and spontaneous breath that moves in and out of your body effortlessly. It flows through both the nostrils. Notice the feeling of the breath as it comes in and out of your nostrils. Notice the sense of coolness as you inhale the breath. Follow the sensation of the breath into the nose, into the body, the back of the throat and the lungs.

[5 seconds pause]

There is sense of warmth as you exhale the breath. Feel this warmth travel upwards on the exhale and feel it on the upper lip. The space between the nose and the mouth as you breath out, exhaling. The natural breath travel through both nostrils in the inhale and the exhale.

[5 seconds pause]

Allowing your breath to become softer and longer. Each breath soft and long, fluid and steady. Taking a long slow inhale followed by a longer slower exhale. Allow you exhale to be even slower, even longer. Notice the slight pause after the exhale a natural moment of stillness. Slow inhale, long soft exhale, and pause. Slow inhale, long soft exhale, and pause. Continue breathing like this for few more moment.

Let go of control on every inhale and exhale. The body knows exactly what to do. Allowing the breath to flow fluidly one breath after the other.

[5 seconds pause]

It is now time to state your resolve – "I have quit smoking forever. I no longer crave for a cigarette. I am a non-smoker." Repeat your inner resolve three times now with full attention.

"I have quit smoking forever. I no longer crave for a cigarette. I am a non-smoker." "I have quit smoking forever. I no longer crave for a cigarette. I am a non-smoker." "I have quit smoking forever. I no longer crave for a cigarette. I am a non-smoker."

[5 seconds pause]

We will now begin a systematic journey of sensory awareness through the body. Move your awareness to different parts of the body as soon as you hear the name, just state the name or the part to yourself and sense into the feeling and that part of your body but do not move your body. Simply follow the guidance with your awareness. And if during the body scan, you find your mind wandering away, gently bring it back and continue with the scan. Becoming aware of the tip of the right hand thumb, right second finger, third finger, fourth finger, palm of the right hand , back of the right hand, right wrist, forearm, right elbow, upper arm, right shoulder, right armpit, right waist, right hip, right thigh, right knee, right calf, right ankle, right heel, sole of the right foot, top of the right foot, right big toe, second toe, third toe, fourth toe, fifth toe.

[5 seconds pause]

Tip of the left hand thumb, second finger, third finger, fourth finger, fifth finger, palm of the left hand, back of the left hand, right wrist, forearm, left elbow, upper arm, left shoulder, left armpit, left waist, left hip, left thigh, left knee, left calf, left ankle, left heel, sole of the left foot, top of the left foot, left big toe, second toe, third toe, fourth toe, fifth toe. And if during the body scan, you find your mind wandering away, gently bring it back and continue with the scan.

Now go to the back of the body. Right heel , left heel. Right calf, left calf.Right thigh, left thigh.Right buttock, left buttock. Lower back, middle back, upper back , the entire spine. And if during the body scan, you find your mind wandering away, gently bring it back and continue with the scan. The right shoulder blade, left shoulder blade. Back of the neck, back of the head, top of the head, forehead. Right temple, left temple, right ear, left ear. Right eyebrow, left eyebrow, center of the eyebrows.

[5 seconds pause]

Right eye, left eye, right nostril, left nostril. Right cheek, left cheek, upper lip, lower lip, both lips together.

[5 seconds pause]

Chin, jaw, throat, right color bone, left color bone. And if during the body scan, you find your mind wandering away, gently bring it back and continue with the scan. Right side of the chest, left side of the chest, upper abdomen, navel, lower abdomen.

[5 seconds pause]

The pelvic floor , the whole right leg, the whole left leg, the whole right arm, the whole left arm, the whole face, the whole head, the whole torso, the whole body, the whole body together. And if during the body scan, you find your mind wandering away, gently bring it back and continue with the scan.

[5 seconds pause]

Now gently bringing your attention to fluid flow of the breath as it moves through the body. Imagine that the breath is flowing along a spinal cord and a milky white stream on the base of the spine to the crown of the head.

[5 seconds pause]

Begin counting down from 12 to 0 with awareness. Move from the root of the base of the spine to the crown at the top of the head. Inhale root to crown, 12. Exhale 11, crown to root. Inhale 10, root to crown. Exhale 9, crown to root. Continue breathing and counting in this way inhale through the breathing to the base of the spine up to the top of the head. Exhale from the top of head to the base of the spine.

[30 seconds pause]

Now let go of the counting. Return to natural breathing; each natural breath flowing through the one after the other.

[5 seconds pause]

Each breath is soft and long, fluid and steady. Now move on to the sensations of the opposites. Now imagine the whole body becoming light. The whole body light, as your whole body could float away from the floor towards the ceiling.

[5 seconds pause]

The head is light and weightless. The limbs are light weightless. The torso is light and weightless.

[5 seconds pause]

The whole body is light and weightless. You are rising higher and higher away from the floor, the whole body light. The whole body light.

[5 seconds pause]

Now I want you to imagine your body becoming heavy. Feel the heaviness on all parts of the body. Each part is becoming heavier and heavier, and heavier. The head is heavy, the limbs are heavy, and the torso heavy, the whole body is heavy as it is sinking down into the floor. The whole body heavy.

[5 seconds pause]

And now awaken the experience of cold in the body. The sensation of coldness , the experience of chilly cold. Imagine being outside in winter out a coat. Feel this chilling wave throughout your body. The whole chilly, chilly cold.

[5 seconds pause]

Now allow the sensation of warmth. Just spread through the entire body. The whole feeling warmth. Remember the feeling of the heat in the summer when you are outside in the sun with no shades. Feel the warmth of the sun radiating on your skin. Heat all around the body. Whole body warm.

[5 seconds pause]

Recall the experience of sadness, intense sadness and longing. Feel the weight of the sadness in your heart and body; don't concentrate on its source. Simply notice the sensations of sadness. Create the experience of sadness as clearly as possible. Deeply feel the experience of sadness.

[5 seconds pause]

Now recall the experience of joy, intense joy and connection, lightness and love. Feel the expensive sensation of joy in your heart and mind but don't concentrate on its source. Create the experience of joy as clearly as possible. Feeling the experience of joy.

[5 seconds pause]

Now allow the feeling of complete calm. Manifest the experience of calm into your entire mind, body and emotions. Experience the sensation of calm. You are relaxed and aware, you are completely calm. Feel the experience of calm in your whole body. The whole body and mind is experiencing calmness.

[20 seconds pause]

Now begin the practice of visualization. Begin to notice the space between your closed eyelids; the space in front of your closed eyelids. Allow yourself to rest your tension here on the space in front of your closed eyelids.

[5 seconds pause]

I want you to imagine before you a transparent screen, much like the screen you might find in a movie theatre. The screen is high and as wide as the eyes can see. Rest your attention and concentration here on this mind screen. Become more of anything manifest within it, colors, patterns, light, whatever you see is the manifesting state of your mind. Continue to hold the awareness of this space but do not become involved what you see.

[5 seconds pause]

Practice detached awareness only. Simply witnessing and observing this brain of the mind. If any subtle images make them so involve simply notice them without directing and engaging. Observing a mind screen.

[5 seconds pause]

Now a number of different things will be named and vision this on the level of emotions. Memory and imagination as best you can and jump from image to image as soon as you hear it, pink desert, peacock feather, a dentist's clinic, a blue square, good night rest, the full moon, your reflection in a mirror. A clear, cloudless, morning, a clear pond, waiting for test results, a gold star, the sun shining overhead, bouquet of flowers. Tall oak tree, helping others, cool clear water, laughing with family, a loving embrace, burning flame, the temple on a mountain, vibrant sunset, taking a deep breath, cant stretching in a beam of sun light. Beautiful garden path, cloudless sky, your body lying on the floor, your body lying on the floor, your breath flowing fluidly and easily. Each breath flowing fluidly one after the other.

[20 seconds pause]

Now I want you to repeat to yourself your resolve thrice. This time, feel it much more deeply than the last time.

[5 seconds pause]

"I have quit smoking forever. I no longer crave for a cigarette. I am a non-smoker." "I have quit smoking forever. I no longer crave for a cigarette. I am a non-smoker." "I have quit smoking forever. I no longer crave for a cigarette. I am a non-smoker."

[10 seconds pause]

Now become aware of the inner space. The inner space you see behind your forehead. Develop your awareness of this space and infinites space that extends as far you can see; as low and as high, as wide and as long as you can see.

[5 seconds pause]

Becoming aware the infinite space of behind your forehead. Become aware of this infinite space. Be totally aware but not involved. Observe this space as if you are watching a movie, what you see is projection of your subconscious. If you see patterns this is simply the way your mind is manifesting. Continue to hold your awareness, simply observing. Be aware of all that is now present in your awareness.

[5 seconds pause]

Feeling yourself is the one who is aware of everything that is present, sensing what's present. Then experiencing yourself as the awareness of everything arising. Dissolve into being pure awareness itself, open and spacious.

[5 seconds pause]

Being awareness in which everything is coming and going. Awareness in which everything is welcome just as it is. Watching, witnessing with no involvement. Continue watching, witnessing this infinite space and silence for a while.

[2 minutes]

It's now time to repeat your resolve one more time. Feel it as if it is the ultimate truth.

"I have quit smoking forever. I no longer crave for a cigarette. I am a non-smoker." "I have quit smoking forever. I no longer crave for a cigarette. I am a non-smoker." "I have quit smoking forever. I no longer crave for a cigarette. I am a non-smoker."

[10 seconds pause]

Return to the feeling of your breath flowing in and out from your nostrils. Feeling the breath moving in and out through the nose. Maintain your awareness of breath for a while.

[20 seconds pause]

Imagine waking up tomorrow and not feeling the craving to smoke. Still out of sheer habit you reach out to your pack of cigarettes, take one out and hold it in your hand. But you don't feel like smoking. You just don't want to put this cigarette in your mouth. And it dawns upon you may be it's the beginning your new smoke-free life. And you start your day in your usual fashion. You will visualise performing all your morning rituals, getting started with day and going about your business but with just one exception – you don't smoke at all. So, I want you to visualise yourself spending the highlights of your day without feeling the need to smoke a single cigarette. You can start the visualisation now

[2 minutes pause]

So how does it feel having spent your entire day without having to smoke a single cigarette? And if you are still left with some part of your day, I will give you one more minute to complete the visualisation or do it one more time if you would like to.

[1 minute pause]

So, come back to my voice. How was your experience? It felt good, didn't it? You must be feeling so proud of yourself to have spent the entire day without smoking a single cigarette. That's surely an achievement. You have every right to feel good about this. And you can go through this day again feeling the special moments. Being happy, being content. It feels so wonderful, almost magical. You have spent your entire day without smoking a cigarette. It surely calls for celebration – but celebration without a cigarette.

And you wake up the next day and you know you have to enjoy this day as a non-smoker to the fullest. So, you start your day by taking long and deep breaths, filling your lungs completely. And it all feels so good. You enjoy each breath as you inhale the fresh air, hold it in your lungs for a moment and then exhale fully. It feels so pleasant. You have never felt so alive before. Every breath you take as a non-smoker feels magical. The air is fresh. It energises you. It rejuvenates you. It helps you see the beauty of being in the moment. You don't crave for a cigarette to start your day. Earlier it might be your habit to look for a cigarette first thing in the morning. But you are no longer a slave of those cigarettes. You are the master of your life. You have made a decision to be a non-smoker and you are sticking to it effortlessly. And you can see the positive changes in your health and wellbeing. You feel so fit and healthy. You have so much energy now. You accomplish all your tasks productively and you don't crave for smoking a cigarette. You no longer feel stressed out. You have realised that having a cigarette to ease stress was an excuse. You have learnt to effectively manage your stress without burning a cigarette – and that feels so great. You are now in complete control of your life. You no longer feel the urge to smoke when experience stress. Stress seems to be a thing of the past now.

[10 seconds pause]

Now imagine waking up next week and feeling even better because it's been one full week without you having touched a cigarette. You feel so proud. It feels as if you are gaining control over your emotions. May be it's the beginning of a beautiful journey, you wonder to yourself. You wonder what if you could keep up the momentum. And you decide to stay away from cigarettes. You can see that you haven't lost the good feelings of smoking. You still feel the pleasures you used to get from smoking but now you feel the same naturally.

[10 seconds pause]

Now, fast forward a month. And you wake up as a non-smoker, feeling even better. You left behind the habit for smoking for good. The best thing is that you haven't had any withdrawal symptoms. The transition has been organic and natural. You haven't forced anything upon yourself. Change is happening naturally. And you are enjoying every moment of this new life. You have this feeling that there's so much in store for you. And you are genuinely happy for this new life as a non-smoker. There's no craving. You are in complete control. And you also notice that your productivity at work has increased manifold. Your focus has multiplied. Your output has increased manifold. You feel so good about everything. Life is so beautiful when you are healthy and happy.

[10 seconds pause]

Now, imagine yourself waking up six months from now. You know you have finally quit smoking forever. You have got your rid of something that had been troubling you for so long. How good do you feel now? Feel the feelings. See from the eyes of the non-smoker you. Listen from the ears. Your personality has changed so much. You are now much more calm and confident. You are happily socialising with people around you, and when someone offers you a cigarette, you confidently look into their eyes and politely reply, "No, thank you, I have quit smoking – haven't smoked a cigarette for the past six months." And they are so impressed by your confidence. They can see the sparkle in your eyes. Your demeanour is so impressive. You are enjoying your freedom as a non-smoker. You know how to be fun without the need to smoke.

[10 seconds pause]

Now, imagine waking up one year from now. You are a completely changed person. You know that as a non-smoker, you can live your life more freely, more actively. You will be the one in charge of your life. You will be free of this habit of smoking. You have realized that being a non-smoker means living a healthy life. You will be much more productive and effective. You are at the peak of your health and fitness. And you can see the positive changes in your health and wellbeing. You feel so fit and healthy. You have so much energy now. You accomplish all your tasks productively and you don't crave for smoking a cigarette. You no longer feel stressed out. You have realised that having a cigarette to ease stress was an excuse. You have learnt to effectively manage your stress without burning a cigarette – and that feels so great. You are now in complete control of your life. You no longer feel the urge to smoke when experience stress. In fact, you hardly feel stressed nowadays and if there's a thing or two that worries you a bit you have found healthy ways to cope up. You are still enjoying all the good feelings you once associated with cigarette and at the same time you lead a healthy, stress-free life of a non-smoker. This is the life you have always wanted to live.

People enjoy your company. They see you as an inspiration to quit smoking. Everything you have always wanted to be, you are now because of your decision to quit smoking. You can stay here a little bit longer and continue with your visualisation for as long as you want. Thank you!

III. Quit Smoking Affirmations

1. Quit Smoking Affirmations – I (40 minutes)

Welcome to this session on affirmations to quit smoking. You can lie down or sit in a comfortable position. We will practice the affirmations after we have relaxed our body so that our subconscious mind is in a more receptive state. Your subconscious mind will itself find ways to make you achieve your goal to quit smoking quite effortlessly. So let's begin by first doing a simple body scan for relaxation.

Take few deep breaths. Taking a big breath in through the nose and releasing through the mouth. In through the nose and out through the mouth. Now allow the breath to return to natural rhythm.

[5 seconds pause]

We will begin our scan of body. Beginning with the left foot and in whatever position it may be noticing any surfaces that the foot may come into contact with. Whether it's a floor, clothing may be bed or blanket, then letting the awareness move over each of the toes. Notice where they may come in contact with one another and the spot where the toes connected to the rest of the foot. And as if the awareness is the spot light, letting this spotlight move up to the sole of the foot. Noticing any sensations whether they be good or bad or neutral. Just taking this moment to tune to these sensations. During the body scan, if your mind wanders, don't worry. Just acknowledge that it has wandered and gently bring your awareness back to the present moment.

[5 seconds pause]

Moving the awareness to the top side to the foot. Now moving on to the left ankle and letting this spot light of the awareness to travel all over the ankle. In a circular slow motion. Noticing every part of the ankle .moving up to the left calf and the left shin.

Feel any sensation or tiredness on your calf and shin. Release it and let go.

[5 seconds pause]

Now move your awareness to your left knee, left thigh feel any sensation there. Now move up to left hip, hip muscles, joints and left side as a whole. This is the area in which we hold lot of tension and stress. Release all the tension and let go. Now take your left side as a whole. What is it like to pay this type of awareness to one part of the body, to give detailed attentions, to this one part of this whole?

[5 seconds pause]

Now draw your awareness to the right side, right foot. Let your awareness drift over each toe. Feel any sensation or tingling, any kind of tension. And then to the place where toes connect to the foot. Let go of all the tensions.

[5 seconds pause]

Now move your awareness to The sole of the right foot. And the top side of the right foot. Then allowing the awareness to circle around the right ankle. Noticing as minute sensations as you can may be even noticing where the skin makes contact with the air or clothing around it. During the body scan, if your mind wanders, don't worry. Just acknowledge that it has wandered and gently bring your awareness back to the present moment. Moving up to the right calf, and the right shin, the right knee, and the right thigh and hamstrings, feel any sensation or tension and let go and release. And now take your right side as a whole, from the toes to the right hip joint.

[5 seconds pause]

Now move up to the body to pelvis. Using the awareness to examine what is felt at the both hips and the spaces between them. The stomach, noticing any sensation on the skin, noticing any tension associated with the breath, or anything else.

[5 seconds pause]

Shift your awareness up to the chest. Perhaps even noticing or you can feel the beat of your heart. and then moving to the back , using this spot light of the awareness to start at the lower back. Slowly scan up the spine. What is this skin making contact with and can you feel it. Are there any sensations within the body? Big or small sensations paying them both equal attentions. During the body scan, if your mind wanders, don't worry. Just acknowledge that it has wandered and gently bring your awareness back to the present moment.

[5 seconds pause]

Then move the awareness to the right shoulder, the right upper arm both front and the back side both biceps and triceps. Feel any sensation there. Feel it and let it go.

[5 seconds pause]

Now let the awareness circle around the elbow. Allow your awareness to shift to your forearm and your right wrist, the right palm and the back side of your right hand. Feel any stress or tension and take a deep breath and let that stress go.

[5 seconds pause]

Now let the spotlight of your awareness thoroughly travel over your each finger of your right hand from the little finger over to the right thumb. Feel any tingling sensation or warmth, let go and release all the sensations. Then noticing the right arm as a whole, noticing its weight, noticing where it may contact with other surfaces or with on body.

[5 seconds pause]

Then let the awareness drift over to the left shoulder. It is a spot where normally we carry lot of tension. Feel your left upper arm, both front and back side, both biceps and triceps. Allow the awareness to circle around the left elbow, and the left forearm, the left wrist, the palm of the left hand, the back side of the left hand, and then allowing the awareness to move over each finger of the left hand slowly. Starting with the little finger drifting over to the thumb. And noticing the full length of the left arm. From shoulder to finger tips. Release all the tensions which you have carried on your left arm. Let go of it. During the body scan, if your mind wanders, don't worry. Just acknowledge that it has wandered and gently bring your awareness back to the present moment.

[5 seconds pause]

Move the spot light of your awareness up to your neck. Noticing the back side where the spine extends upwards. And noticing the front side of the neck beneath the chin. Notice any tension or tiredness there. Release it, let go of it. Move the awareness up to the jaw. Notice where the jaw hold any tension. Take a deep breath and allow all the tension to release.

[5 seconds pause]

Now move your awareness to your lips. Whether they make contact with one another or perhaps noticing the air between them if they are separated? Notice each check of your face. And draw awareness to your nose, to your nostrils as they breathe in all day and night the fresh air for your lungs. Notice any awareness there and allow them to release.

[5 seconds pause]

Noticing the sensation of breaths. Moving in and out through the nose or through the lips and then the eyes, the brow and the forehead. During the body scan, if your mind wanders, don't worry. Just acknowledge that it has wandered and gently bring your awareness back to the present moment. And then taking the time to move this spotlight of awareness to your left ear and then your right ear. Feel any tension and release.

Draw your awareness to your scalp, from the base of your skull to the crown of your head. Feel any heaviness or stress. Release all the stress and fill your crown with peace and calmness. During the body scan, if your mind wanders, don't worry. Just acknowledge that it has wandered and gently bring your awareness back to the present moment. Now slowly moving this awareness to encompass the whole body, beginning with the crown of the head, down through the face, the neck, the left arm, the right arm, the back, the chest, the belly, the pelvis, the right leg and the left leg, allow your awareness to rest on this whole body. Scan your body again, if you still feel any tiredness or tension remain in your body, you can let them go now.

[2 minutes]

Now we are going to begin with the affirmations, saying each one thrice. Saying an intention or affirmation has a deep-rooted impact on our subconscious mind. So, let's start now. Repeat after me.

I have quit smoking forever. The decision to quit smoking has been the best decision of my life. I have adjusted beautifully in my new life as a non-smoker. The transformation into the non-smoker has opened so many doors of opportunities. I enjoy every moment of health and wellbeing. I am grateful and happy.

[5 seconds]

I have quit smoking forever. The decision to quit smoking has been the best decision of my life. I have adjusted beautifully in my new life as a non-smoker. The transformation into the non-smoker has opened so many doors of opportunities. I enjoy every moment of health and wellbeing. I am grateful and happy.

[5 seconds]

I have quit smoking forever. The decision to quit smoking has been the best decision of my life. I have adjusted beautifully in my new life as a non-smoker. The transformation into the non-smoker has opened so many doors of opportunities. I enjoy every moment of health and wellbeing. I am grateful and happy.

[10 seconds pause]

My mind and body are strong enough. I have the inherent strength to quit smoking forever. I no longer feel the craving to smoke. I am stronger than a cigarette. I am in control of my mind, emotions, and thoughts. I am getting stronger with each passing day.

[5 seconds]

My mind and body are strong enough. I have the inherent strength to quit smoking forever. I no longer feel the craving to smoke. I am stronger than a cigarette. I am in control of my mind, emotions, and thoughts. I am getting stronger with each passing day.

[5 seconds]

My mind and body are strong enough. I have the inherent strength to quit smoking forever. I no longer feel the craving to smoke. I am stronger than a cigarette. I am in control of my mind, emotions, and thoughts. I am getting stronger with each passing day.

[10 seconds pause]

Now I feel so happy and pleasant. My life has changed completely for the better. New opportunities are coming my way. I am more receptive and sensitive to the good things in life. Quitting smoking has brought so many beautiful changes in my life. I am grateful to have made this decision.

[5 seconds]

Now I feel so happy and pleasant. My life has changed completely for the better. New opportunities are coming my way. I am more receptive and sensitive to the good things in life. Quitting smoking has brought so many beautiful changes in my life. I am grateful to have made this decision.

[5 seconds]

Now I feel so happy and pleasant. My life has changed completely for the better. New opportunities are coming my way. I am more receptive and sensitive to the good things in life. Quitting smoking has brought so many beautiful changes in my life. I am grateful to have made this decision.

[10 seconds pause]

I enjoy a healthy lifestyle. I eat nourishing food and drink a lot of water. I exercise and take of my health. Since I have quit smoking my stamina has improved substantially. Everything in my life is falling in place. I am at my ideal shape and size.

[5 seconds]

I enjoy a healthy lifestyle. I eat nourishing food and drink a lot of water. I exercise and take of my health. Since I have quit smoking my stamina has improved substantially. Everything in my life is falling in place. I am at my ideal shape and size

[5 seconds]

I enjoy a healthy lifestyle. I eat nourishing food and drink a lot of water. I exercise and take of my health. Since I have quit smoking my stamina has improved substantially. Everything in my life is falling in place. I am at my ideal shape and size

[10 seconds pause]

My skin glows with radiance and beauty. My eyes sparkle with unmistakable confidence. My physical body looks exactly I want it to be. People are always complementing me on how much good I look now. The changes that I have on the inside are also showing positively on the outside. I am comfortable and confident in my body.

[5 seconds]

My skin glows with radiance and beauty. My eyes sparkle with unmistakable confidence. My physical body looks exactly I want it to be. People are always complementing me on how much good I look now. The changes that I have on the inside are also showing positively on the outside. I am comfortable and confident in my body.

[5 seconds]

My skin glows with radiance and beauty. My eyes sparkle with unmistakable confidence. My physical body looks exactly I want it to be. People are always complementing me on how much good I look now. The changes that I have on the inside are also showing positively on the outside. I am comfortable and confident in my body.

[10 seconds pause]

Having quit smoking, I now find myself more productive at work. I feel that I now have more time and energy to complete my tasks effectively. Everyone around me is appreciating my work quality and performance. I am being rewarded for my improved performance and initiatives. Every day is full of new achievements. I am at my productive best.

[5 seconds]

Having quit smoking, I now find myself more productive at work. I feel that I now have more time and energy to complete my tasks effectively. Everyone around me is appreciating my work quality and performance. I am being rewarded for my improved performance and initiatives. Every day is full of new achievements. I am at my productive best.

[5 seconds]

Having quit smoking, I now find myself more productive at work. I feel that I now have more time and energy to complete my tasks effectively. Everyone around me is appreciating my work quality and performance. I am being rewarded for my improved performance and initiatives. Every day is full of new achievements. I am at my productive best.

[10 seconds pause]

This new life as a non-smoker is much more fun and exciting. People love to hang out with me. I am enjoying the confidence that comes with being a non-smoker. I now enjoy life more fully and freely. Every day of life is now full of excitement. I often get complemented that I am fun to be around.

[5 seconds]

This new life as a non-smoker is much more fun and exciting. People love to hang out with me. I am enjoying the confidence that comes with being a non-smoker. I now enjoy life more fully and freely. Every day of life is now full of excitement. I often get complemented that I am fun to be around.

[5 seconds]

This new life as a non-smoker is much more fun and exciting. People love to hang out with me. I am enjoying the confidence that comes with being a non-smoker. I now enjoy life more fully and freely. Every day of life is now full of excitement. I often get complemented that I am fun to be around.

[10 seconds pause]

I am in complete control of my emotions. I don't feel the craving to smoke. I am the master of my ship. I have control over my feelings. I am in charge of my life. I know what's best for me and act accordingly. The decision to quit smoking has given me clarity and control over life.

[5 seconds]

I am in complete control of my emotions. I don't feel the craving to smoke. I am the master of my ship. I have control over my feelings. I am in charge of my life. I know what's best for me and act accordingly. The decision to quit smoking has given me clarity and control over life.

[5 seconds]

I am in complete control of my emotions. I don't feel the craving to smoke. I am the master of my ship. I have control over my feelings. I am in charge of my life. I know what's best for me and act accordingly. The decision to quit smoking has given me clarity and control over life.

[10 seconds pause]

My mind now feels so much calm and relaxed. I am balanced at all times. I take care of my mental wellbeing. I know how to effectively manage stress and anxiety. My mental health has improved so much after quitting cigarettes. I have the mental strength to overcome all challenges of life.

[5 seconds]

My mind now feels so much calm and relaxed. I am balanced at all times. I take care of my mental wellbeing. I know how to effectively manage stress and anxiety. My mental health has improved so much after quitting cigarettes. I have the mental strength to overcome all challenges of life.

[5 seconds]

My mind now feels so much calm and relaxed. I am balanced at all times. I take care of my mental wellbeing. I know how to effectively manage stress and anxiety. My mental health has improved so much after quitting cigarettes. I have the mental strength to overcome all challenges of life.

[10 seconds pause]

I am the happiest being a non-smoker. The decision to quit smoking has been the most fruitful and helpful decision of my life. I like the changes that are happening in my life. I enjoy every moment of my life. I have much more time to pursue hobbies and do things that I had always wanted to do. I am happy and satisfied with my decision to quit smoking.

[5 seconds]

I am the happiest being a non-smoker. The decision to quit smoking has been the most fruitful and helpful decision of my life. I like the changes that are happening in my life. I enjoy every moment of my life. I have much more time to pursue hobbies and do things that I had always wanted to do. I am happy and satisfied with my decision to quit smoking.

[5 seconds]

I am the happiest being a non-smoker. The decision to quit smoking has been the most fruitful and helpful decision of my life. I like the changes that are happening in my life. I enjoy every moment of my life. I have much more time to pursue hobbies and do things that I had always wanted to do. I am happy and satisfied with my decision to quit smoking.

[10 seconds pause]

As I relax, my subconscious mind is rewiring to make me quit smoking. My subconscious mind is looking for ways to make me enjoy the good feelings I used to get from smoking without actually having to smoke a cigarette. I will continue to enjoy the good feelings and at the same time enjoy the long-term health benefits of being a non-smoker. My subconscious mind is reprogramming to quit the unhealthy habit of smoking. My transition into a non-smoker is happening naturally and effortlessly.

[5 seconds]

As I relax, my subconscious mind is rewiring to make me quit smoking. My subconscious mind is looking for ways to make me enjoy the good feelings I used to get from smoking without actually having to smoke a cigarette. I will continue to enjoy the good feelings and at the same time enjoy the long-term health benefits of being a non-smoker. My subconscious mind is reprogramming to quit the unhealthy habit of smoking. My transition into a non-smoker is happening naturally and effortlessly.

[5 seconds]

As I relax, my subconscious mind is rewiring to make me quit smoking. My subconscious mind is looking for ways to make me enjoy the good feelings I used to get from smoking without actually having to smoke a cigarette. I will continue to enjoy the good feelings and at the same time enjoy the long-term health benefits of being a non-smoker. My subconscious mind is reprogramming to quit the unhealthy habit of smoking. My transition into a non-smoker is happening naturally and effortlessly.

2. Quit Smoking Affirmations – II (60 minutes)

Repeating affirmations have a deep-rooted and positive impact on our subconscious mind. Scientific studies have shown that the affirmations become much more effective when practiced with a relaxed state of mind. So, we will begin today's session by relaxing you with a simple meditation and then we will move on to the affirmations.

Close your eyes. Take a few deep breaths in through the nose and out through the mouth.

[15 seconds pause]

Return to your natural effortless breath.

[5 seconds pause]

Feel your body resting into the surface. Feel the body beginning to soften and let go. Notice all the places where your body is supported. Perhaps the heels and backs of the legs and buttocks. Notice where your back head and neck are supported. Trust in your support and safety. Invite softness into your being. Allow the forehead and eyes to soften. Eye heavy and the sockets.

[5 seconds pause]

Invite the jaw to release, perhaps parting the lips or separating the backs of your teeth. Invite the throat, the hard space to begin to soften. The shoulders, arms and hands, fingers, the abdomen, legs and feet. Begin to notice sounds, sense of hearing the sound at the distance. Notice the most distance you can hear. Let each sounds be an anonymous vibration of energy. Listen to the closer sounds now.

[5 seconds pause]

Allowing the awareness to move from sound to sound. Listen to the sound what is happening inside your own body. Focus on the natural sounds of the body. Perhaps you can hear your pulse. Sounds of digestion, heart beating, and gentle sound of your own breath. May be you can sense even more subtle inner sounds.

[5 seconds pause]

Now imagine yourself resting in a place that makes you feel safe and comforted. And may be real imagined, indoors or out. This is a place that offers you peace, comfort and nurturing. Feel yourself here, begin to notice all the surroundings. Any colors, quality of a light, meaningful objects, Plant and animals companions, any spiritual guides. And see yourself here in this peaceful place. Notice how you feel in this place. Be aware of the atmosphere of calm and safety.

[5 seconds pause]

At any time during the practice, you can guide yourself here in your inner sanctuary. If at any times during the practice you find yourself experience any sense of ease or discomfort, your inner sanctuary is here for you.

[5 seconds pause]

Bring your attention to your physical body. I will guide you to systematic scan your body as each body part is named. Draw your attention to that body part. Notice just it is. And in your mind speak the mantra easy and relaxed. We will begin at the right hand side of the body.

[5 seconds pause]

Become aware of the right hand thumb. Notice the right hand thumb say it to yourself easy and relaxed. Continue on this way. First finger, second finger, third finger, fourth finger, palm of the hand, wrist, forearm, elbow, upper arm and shoulder. Side of the torso, waist, hip, thigh, knee, lower leg, ankle, sole of the foot, top of the foot, right big toes, second toe, third toe, fourth toe and the fifth toe. Whole right side of the body, easy and relaxed.

[5 seconds pause]

Shift awareness to the left hand side of the body, left hand thumb, first finger, second finger, third finger, fourth finger, palm of the hand, wrist, forearm, elbow, upper arm and shoulder. Left side of the torso, waist, hip, thigh, knee, lower leg, ankle, sole of the foot, top of the foot, left big toe, second toe, third toe, fourth toe, fifth toe, awareness of the whole left side of the body, easy and relaxed.

[5 seconds pause]

Become aware of the back body now. Notice both heels, both calves, the backs of the thighs, buttocks, the lower back, middle back, shoulder blades, upper back, back of the neck, base of the scalp, back of the head, crown of the head , the whole back body, easy and relaxed.

[5 seconds pause]

Shift awareness to the front body. Forehead, temples, eyebrows, your eyebrow center point. Notice the eyes, eyelids, ears, cheeks, nostrils, lips, tongue, teeth, jaw, chin, front of the neck, throat. Color bones, chest, heart center, upper abdomen, navel center, lower abdomen, pelvis, pelvic floor, front of the thighs, knee capes, shins, feet, the whole front of the body, easy and relaxed.

[5 seconds pause]

Shift your attention to movement of the natural breath. Notice the rise and fall of the belly. The subtle expansion. Release of the ribcage. Feel the gentle wave like motion of the breath. Notice any sensations as you breathe in and as you breathe out. Inhaling and exhaling effortlessly. As you inhale say it to yourself Easy and relaxed and as you exhale say it to yourself I am at peace.

[5 seconds pause]

Let go over the breath and mantra now. At this time in the practice looks for opposites and sensations and emotions. Allow yourself to be with any sensations and emotions that may arise. Know that you are safe to experience the fluctuations in the mind. And that your inner sanctuary is there for you should you need to guide yourself there.

[5 seconds pause]

Imagine your body feels contracted. Your whole being is contracted. Turn inward, perhaps tiny, and tight. Notice sensation of contraction in your being. Whole being is contracted. Release contraction. And in widen the opposite. Feel yourself as expensive, spacious. Notice the outward flow of energy. Whole being is expensive. [5 seconds pause]

Let go of expansion and turn awareness to contraction. Release contraction and return to expansion. Allow the awareness to move back and forth between contractions and opposite. Now see if you can experience both at the same time. Release this.

[5 seconds pause]

Now invite in a limiting belief or emotion that you are working with your life or your spiritual practice. Allow yourself to fully experience this belief or emotion. Feel it in your body, every cell of your being. Now find the opposite emotion or belief. If the initial emotion or belief weren't there. How would you feel? What would you believe?

Allow yourself to fully experience this opposite in your entire being.

[5 seconds pause]

Now feel the emotions or limited belief you are working with again. Now experience the opposite. Allow your awareness to move back and forth between these opposites. Perhaps noticing what happens to these intensities of these opposites. Let the mind move back and forth.

[5 seconds pause]

Now see if you can hold both in your mind at once. Both the limiting belief or emotions and its opposite, all at once. And let it go.

[5 seconds pause]

Shift awareness to the space in front of the closed dice. Gaze into your mind's eye. Invite in all of your senses to bring in the things. Sun rising over red wood trees, The field of lavender, city lights at night, freshly ground coffee, bells ringing in a distance, ancient stone formation, a monolith rock, a pink lotus flower, o log of wood, a cat sleeping in a sun beam, a wise ancestor, a forest of bamboo trees, crickets chirping, a peaceful peasant, constellations of the stars in the night sky. See yourself in a restful meditation. A breath of the universe, expanding into an infinite, infinite awareness, Infinite bliss.

[5 seconds pause]

Relax. Completely relax. Let go of every thought, every worry.

[5 seconds pause]

You are here because you want to quit smoking. The entire universe will conspire to make that happen for you. Have faith and hold on.

[5 seconds pause]

Feel yourself becoming open and free, radiating light and bliss. Become aware of yourself as the observer of your breath, body and breath and intellect. Notice thoughts, feelings and sensations arriving with in your consciousness. Feel in to your breath again. Maintain a gentle awareness on your breath.

[5 minutes]

Let's begin with the affirmations now. Each affirmation will be repeated three times. So, repeat after me with all your focus and intentions.

I am living my life as a non-smoker. I have quit smoking forever. Smoking cigarettes is a thing of the past for me. I save my money, time, and energy as a non-smoker. I have adjusted beautifully in my new life as a non-smoker. I am very happy and satisfied with my decision.

[5 seconds pause]

I am living my life as a non-smoker. I have quit smoking forever. Smoking cigarettes is a thing of the past for me. I save my money, time, and energy as a non-smoker. I have adjusted beautifully in my new life as a non-smoker. I am very happy and satisfied with my decision.

[5 seconds pause]

I am living my life as a non-smoker. I have quit smoking forever. Smoking cigarettes is a thing of the past for me. I save my money, time, and energy as a non-smoker. I have adjusted beautifully in my new life as a non-smoker. I am very happy and satisfied with my decision.

[10 seconds pause]

I have quit smoking effortlessly. The transformation from the 'smoker me' to the 'non-smoker me' has been smooth and successful. I am enjoying the new version of myself. The changes I see in myself are being appreciated by those around me. I am happier and healthier than I ever imagined I could be after I quit smoking. The transition is beautiful and I am enjoying every moment of it.

[5 seconds pause]

I have quit smoking effortlessly. The transformation from the 'smoker me' to the 'non-smoker me' has been smooth and successful. I am enjoying the new version of myself. The changes I see in myself are being appreciated by those around me. I am happier and healthier than I ever imagined I could be after I quit smoking. The transition is beautiful and I am enjoying every moment of it.

[5 seconds pause]

I have quit smoking effortlessly. The transformation from the 'smoker me' to the 'non-smoker me' has been smooth and successful. I am enjoying the new version of myself. The changes I see in myself are being appreciated by those around me. I am happier and healthier than I ever imagined I could be after I quit smoking. The transition is beautiful and I am enjoying every moment of it.

[10 seconds pause]

There have been no negative side effects after I quit smoking. I have embraced and settled into the new life effortlessly.

Everything is working out perfectly for me. The decision to quit smoking has been the best decision of my life. I did not suffer from any withdrawal symptoms. All is well in my life after I quit smoking.

[5 seconds pause]

There have been no negative side effects after I quit smoking. I have embraced and settled into the new life effortlessly. Everything is working out perfectly for me. The decision to quit smoking has been the best decision of my life. I did not suffer from any withdrawal symptoms. All is well in my life after I quit smoking.

[5 seconds pause]

There have been no negative side effects after I quit smoking. I have embraced and settled into the new life effortlessly. Everything is working out perfectly for me. The decision to quit smoking has been the best decision of my life. I did not suffer from any withdrawal symptoms. All is well in my life after I quit smoking.

[10 seconds pause]

My body is a wonderful tool for me to achieve my highest goal. I quit smoking because I honour my body. My body will no longer suffer from the ill-effects of smoking. My body is a temple and I will no longer be poisoning my body with nicotine and tar. My decision to quit smoking stems from the love and respect I have for my body. My body is responding beautifully and is being healed.

[5 seconds pause]

My body is a wonderful tool for me to achieve my highest goal. I quit smoking because I honour my body. My body will no longer suffer from the ill-effects of smoking. My body is a temple and I will no longer be poisoning my body with nicotine and tar. My decision to quit smoking stems from the love and respect I have for my body. My body is responding beautifully and is being healed.

[5 seconds pause]

My body is a wonderful tool for me to achieve my highest goal. I quit smoking because I honour my body. My body will no longer suffer from the ill-effects of smoking. My body is a temple and I will no longer be poisoning my body with nicotine and tar. My decision to quit smoking stems from the love and respect I have for my body. My body is responding beautifully and is being healed.

[10 seconds pause]

I enjoy good health. Every part of my body is being healed. All my cells, organs, and muscles are full of positive energy and good health. I release all the stress and tension from my physical and mental self. My body is being cleansed of all the does not serve me. I have a balanced state of mind.

[5 seconds pause]

I enjoy good health. Every part of my body is being healed. All my cells, organs, and muscles are full of positive energy and good health. I release all the stress and tension from my physical and mental self. My body is being cleansed of all the does not serve me. I have a balanced state of mind.

[5 seconds pause]

I enjoy good health. Every part of my body is being healed. All my cells, organs, and muscles are full of positive energy and good health. I release all the stress and tension from my physical and mental self. My body is being cleansed of all the does not serve me. I have a balanced state of mind.

[10 seconds pause]

My lungs are healthy. My lungs are being cleansed of the tar and harmful residue from smoking. I am completely cleansed and purified. My lungs are working perfectly. I enjoy fresh air entering my lungs. I breathe in freshness and good health.

[5 seconds pause]

My lungs are healthy. My lungs are being cleansed of the tar and harmful residue from smoking. I am completely cleansed and purified. My lungs are working perfectly. I enjoy fresh air entering my lungs. I breathe in freshness and good health.

[5 seconds pause]

My lungs are healthy. My lungs are being cleansed of the tar and harmful residue from smoking. I am completely cleansed and purified. My lungs are working perfectly. I enjoy fresh air entering my lungs. I breathe in freshness and good health.

[10 seconds pause]

My senses have become much more active and sensitive. I can see things much more clearly and with a better perspective. I enjoy the smell of good aroma and fresh air around me. I listen to the music of nature more attentively. I speak with clarity and confidence. I am much more receptive to changes around me.

My senses have become much more active and sensitive. I can see things much more clearly and with a better perspective. I enjoy the smell of good aroma and fresh air around me. I listen to the music of nature more attentively. I speak with clarity and confidence. I am much more receptive to changes around me.

[5 seconds pause]

My senses have become much more active and sensitive. I can see things much more clearly and with a better perspective. I enjoy the smell of good aroma and fresh air around me. I listen to the music of nature more attentively. I speak with clarity and confidence. I am much more receptive to changes around me.

[10 seconds pause]

I have quit smoking but I continue the good feelings used to get from a cigarette. I no longer feel stressed out. I am always calm and peaceful. I am enjoying my life to the fullest. The pleasures of smoking are still there without the need to light up a cigarette. I am enjoying the best of both the worlds.

[5 seconds pause]

I have quit smoking but I continue the good feelings used to get from a cigarette. I no longer feel stressed out. I am always calm and peaceful. I am enjoying my life to the fullest. The pleasures of smoking are still there without the need to light up a cigarette. I am enjoying the best of both the worlds.

[5 seconds pause]

I have quit smoking but I continue the good feelings used to get from a cigarette. I no longer feel stressed out. I am always calm and peaceful. I am enjoying my life to the fullest. The pleasures of smoking are still there without the need to light up a cigarette. I am enjoying the best of both the worlds.

[10 seconds pause]

I feel more active and energetic than ever before. I am alert and aware. As a non-smoker, I engage in every aspect of life with full eagerness and interest. I live my life with much more vigour and enthusiasm. I have realised that there's so much to life than I had ever imagined. This new life as a non-smoker is so much fun.

I feel more active and energetic than ever before. I am alert and aware. As a non-smoker, I engage in every aspect of life with full eagerness and interest. I live my life with much more vigour and enthusiasm. I have realised that there's so much to life than I had ever imagined. This new life as a non-smoker is so much fun.

[5 seconds pause]

I feel more active and energetic than ever before. I am alert and aware. As a non-smoker, I engage in every aspect of life with full eagerness and interest. I live my life with much more vigour and enthusiasm. I have realised that there's so much to life than I had ever imagined. This new life as a non-smoker is so much fun.

[10 seconds pause]

People around me are appreciating the new non-smoker version of me. Everyone is full of praises for my commitment to be a non-smoker. The positive change in me is visible to one and all. I am being viewed as an inspiration for those who are trying to quit smoking. I am thankful that I can bring some positive change in others. I have gained respect in the eyes of those who matter to me.

[5 seconds pause]

People around me are appreciating the new non-smoker version of me. Everyone is full of praises for my commitment to be a non-smoker. The positive change in me is visible to one and all. I am being viewed as an inspiration for those who are trying to quit smoking. I am thankful that I can bring some positive change in others. I have gained respect in the eyes of those who matter to me.

[5 seconds pause]

People around me are appreciating the new non-smoker version of me. Everyone is full of praises for my commitment to be a non-smoker. The positive change in me is visible to one and all. I am being viewed as an inspiration for those who are trying to quit smoking. I am thankful that I can bring some positive change in others. I have gained respect in the eyes of those who matter to me.

[10 seconds pause]

The non-smoker me is full of unmistakable confidence. People around me are being charmed by my charisma. I am so much comfortable and confident when among people. I have this great feeling that I know what I want and how to achieve that goal. I have will-power and self-discipline to achieve any task I put my mind to. I am confident in all spheres of life.

[5 seconds pause]

The non-smoker me is full of unmistakable confidence. People around me are being charmed by my charisma. I am so much comfortable and confident when among people. I have this great feeling that I know what I want and how to achieve that goal. I have will-power and self-discipline to achieve any task I put my mind to. I am confident in all spheres of life.

[5 seconds pause]

The non-smoker me is full of unmistakable confidence. People around me are being charmed by my charisma. I am so much comfortable and confident when among people. I have this great feeling that I know what I want and how to achieve that goal. I have will-power and self-discipline to achieve any task I put my mind to. I am confident in all spheres of life.

[10 seconds pause]

The craving for a cigarette now feels like a thing of the past. I have the strength and willpower to live the rest of my life without touching a cigarette. My cravings for cigarette have ceased naturally. I know how to release stress naturally. I continue to enjoy the good feelings I used to get from smoking without lighting a cigarette. I never ever feel the craving for a cigarette.

[5 seconds pause]

The craving for a cigarette now feels like a thing of the past. I have the strength and willpower to live the rest of my life without touching a cigarette. My cravings for cigarette have ceased naturally. I know how to release stress naturally. I continue to enjoy the good feelings I used to get from smoking without lighting a cigarette. I never ever feel the craving for a cigarette.

[5 seconds pause]

The craving for a cigarette now feels like a thing of the past. I have the strength and willpower to live the rest of my life without touching a cigarette. My cravings for cigarette have ceased naturally. I know how to release stress naturally. I continue to enjoy the good feelings I used to get from smoking without lighting a cigarette. I never ever feel the craving for a cigarette.

[10 seconds pause]

I wake up every day fully refreshed and reinvigorated. I breathe in fresh air and feel grateful for the same. I no longer feel the craving to smoke. I am excited about what the day holds for me. Throughout the day, I can feel the flow of positive energy inside of me. Being a non-smoker has filled my life with new opportunities. I go to bed every night feeling fulfilled and blessed.

[5 seconds pause]

I wake up every day fully refreshed and reinvigorated. I breathe in fresh air and feel grateful for the same. I no longer feel the craving to smoke. I am excited about what the day holds for me. Throughout the day, I can feel the flow of positive energy inside of me. Being a non-smoker has filled my life with new opportunities. I go to bed every night feeling fulfilled and blessed.

[5 seconds pause]

I wake up every day fully refreshed and reinvigorated. I breathe in fresh air and feel grateful for the same. I no longer feel the craving to smoke. I am excited about what the day holds for me. Throughout the day, I can feel the flow of positive energy inside of me. Being a non-smoker has filled my life with new opportunities. I go to bed every night feeling fulfilled and blessed.

[10 seconds pause]

I have successfully quit smoking without any harmful side effects. My health has been improving with each passing day. My lungs and my entire body are being cleansed of the harmful chemicals of smoking. My life has changed for the better. The decision to quit smoking has been the best decision of my life. I didn't face any withdrawal symptoms after quitting cigarette.

[5 seconds pause]

I have successfully quit smoking without any harmful side effects. My health has been improving with each passing day. My lungs and my entire body are being cleansed of the harmful chemicals of smoking. My life has changed for the better. The decision to quit smoking has been the best decision of my life. I didn't face any withdrawal symptoms after quitting cigarette.

[5 seconds pause]

I have successfully quit smoking without any harmful side effects. My health has been improving with each passing day. My lungs and my entire body are being cleansed of the harmful chemicals of smoking. My life has changed for the better. The decision to quit smoking has been the best decision of my life. I didn't face any withdrawal symptoms after quitting cigarette.

[10 seconds pause]

I love the non-smoker me. I am at peace with myself. I am happy and cheerful throughout the day. My life is now so much beautiful and full of happiness. I now create so many memories with my family and friends. I am loving this new life of a non-smoker.

[5 seconds pause]

I love the non-smoker me. I am at peace with myself. I am happy and cheerful throughout the day. My life is now so much beautiful and full of happiness. I now create so many memories with my family and friends. I am loving this new life of a non-smoker.

[5 seconds pause]

I love the non-smoker me. I am at peace with myself. I am happy and cheerful throughout the day. My life is now so much beautiful and full of happiness. I now create so many memories with my family and friends. I am loving this new life of a non-smoker.

[10 seconds pause]

I am emotionally balanced. I longer depend on cigarettes to feel better. I release stress naturally without smoking a cigarette. I am much more in control of my emotions. I know how to express myself. I am at peace with myself. I enjoy emotional stability. I can handle all situations of life.

[5 seconds pause]

I am emotionally balanced. I longer depend on cigarettes to feel better. I release stress naturally without smoking a cigarette. I am much more in control of my emotions. I know how to express myself. I am at peace with myself. I enjoy emotional stability. I can handle all situations of life.

[5 seconds pause]

I am emotionally balanced. I longer depend on cigarettes to feel better. I release stress naturally without smoking a cigarette. I am much more in control of my emotions. I know how to express myself. I am at peace with myself. I enjoy emotional stability. I can handle all situations of life.

[10 seconds pause]

I take care of my health and fitness. I eat nutritious food and drink a lot of water. I exercise on a regular basis. I eat a balanced and healthy diet. I have achieved and maintained my ideal weight and size. I have made fitness a part of my daily routine. I take good care of my physical and mental health.

[5 seconds pause]

I take care of my health and fitness. I eat nutritious food and drink a lot of water. I exercise on a regular basis. I eat a balanced and healthy diet. I have achieved and maintained my ideal weight and size. I have made fitness a part of my daily routine. I take good care of my physical and mental health.

[5 seconds pause]

I take care of my health and fitness. I eat nutritious food and drink a lot of water. I exercise on a regular basis. I eat a balanced and healthy diet. I have achieved and maintained my ideal weight and size. I have made fitness a part of my daily routine. I take good care of my physical and mental health.

[10 seconds pause]

My subconscious mind is finding out ways to make me quit smoking. I will automatically find myself making healthier life choices. I no longer crave for cigarettes. My subconscious mind knows how to keep the good feelings I get from cigarette without me having to ever smoke again. My subconscious mind is rewiring to make me change my habits and become a non-smoker.

[5 seconds pause]

My subconscious mind is finding out ways to make me quit smoking. I will automatically find myself making healthier life choices. I no longer crave for cigarettes. My subconscious mind knows how to keep the good feelings I get from cigarette without me having to ever smoke again. My subconscious mind is rewiring to make me change my habits and become a non-smoker.

[5 seconds pause]

My subconscious mind is finding out ways to make me quit smoking. I will automatically find myself making healthier life choices. I no longer crave for cigarettes. My subconscious mind knows how to keep the good feelings I get from cigarette without me having to ever smoke again. My subconscious mind is rewiring to make me change my habits and become a non-smoker.

[10 seconds pause]

I feel so grateful for having made the decision to quit smoking. I have the required strength and power to remain a non-smoker for the rest of my life. Many beautiful changes have happened in my personal and professional life ever since I quit smoking. I now have gained my control back over my life. I am in charge of my life and I take full responsibility for my actions.

[5 seconds pause]

I feel so grateful for having made the decision to quit smoking. I have the required strength and power to remain a non-smoker for the rest of my life. Many beautiful changes have happened in my personal and professional life ever since I quit smoking. I now have gained my control back over my life. I am in charge of my life and I take full responsibility for my actions.

[5 seconds pause]

I feel so grateful for having made the decision to quit smoking. I have the required strength and power to remain a non-smoker for the rest of my life. Many beautiful changes have happened in my personal and professional life ever since I quit smoking. I now have gained my control back over my life. I am in charge of my life and I take full responsibility for my actions.

IV. Quit Smoking Hypnosis

1. Quit Smoking Hypnosis – I (50 minutes)

You are about to enter a state of hypnotic trance. Do not listen to this audio when you are operating heavy machinery or doing something that requires your attention. You should preferably be lying down or sitting comfortably on your bed, sofa, or a mat. This hypnosis should best be enjoyed using headphones. By the time you reach the end of this audio, you will wake up completely relaxed and reinvigorated.

So, close your eyes and let go of any thoughts that have been troubling you. This time is solely for your healing. Listen to my voice with full focus and follow my instructions. If your mind wanders during the course of the hypnosis, gently bring it back. Right now, you need to simply relax and let go of any thoughts. Loosen up your body. First I will be relaxing your physical body to make it easier for your subconscious mind to follow my instructions and act on it. So, let's begin.

Allow yourself, invite yourself to enter in this moment and to connect with the body; the body that is your constant companion. Present in this moment and observing that the attention whatever it is arises. Some people notice that they feel very relaxed during the exercise and some people don't. Whatever you experience you invited to welcome it and become curious about it. So allowing yourself to just be here with nowhere you have to go, nothing that you must achieve. No else in this moment to have to please. No right way to feel.

[5 seconds pause]

Settle in the body with the intention to let go of the emotions and thoughts that no longer serve you. Become aware of any particular thoughts that might be present or emotions. Noticing any impatience or burden or perhaps excitement is around. And allow the attention to move to the points where the body is making contact, the surface that you are on. Feeling how the body is carried by the surface. Feeling how gravity forces the body down towards the ground. If you want giving yourself over letting go. Being held and you might become aware of how the breath is moving in and out from the body, it might be shallow or deep, might be fast or slow. And without even trying the breath just flows in and flows out. And you might notice that how the belly moves up and down with each breath. And if you want to lie deepen and invite the breath, to go just little bit deeper, little bit slower, little bit fuller. And if any time the attention wonders away, the Moment you notice it, it's a Moment of mindfulness. And you can just gentle invite the attention to the present moment. Becoming curious of what's here now.

[5 seconds pause]

So allow the body with each out breath to let go. Then moving the attention like a spotlight from the of breath of the belly done into the left leg and all the way to the left big toe and becoming more curious you have ever been before about this big left toes. What sensations are present or perhaps not present, perhaps you feel something or perhaps you don't. There might be Tingling or pulsing or warmth or may be cold. Welcoming whatever it is that you have discover. Perhaps even imagining as you be then how the breath moves into this body part. And as you breathe out letting go. Being the attention to the pinky toe, left pinky toe and allows to toes in between. What is that here to notice. Here in the toes on the left foot. And the toes can be still and with the attention exploring, noticing , welcoming what you need and then allowing the breath to flow in down into the toes and then back out. Letting go.

[5 seconds pause]

Move the attention to the sole of the left foot. Noticing whatever there is here in the sole of the left foot. Perhaps the feel of fabric touching the foot or something else. It's your experience. Breathing into the sole of the foot and then letting go. Bringing the attention to the top of the foot and then to the left heel. May be there is a feel of the ground beneath the left heel. Pressure or sink something completely different.

[5 seconds pause]

And then bring your attention to the heel to the whole left foot. Noticing how the attention can be focused, make a pin point or more expensive the whole left foot and massive sensations, temperature energy.

[5 seconds pause]

Imagine the breath moving into the left foot. And the letting go with the left foot. Shift the attention to the left ankle. Notice anything that's here to be discovered. Move your attention to the lower left leg, the calf, the shin, the muscles and the bone in between. What do you notice here in this moment, different than any other moment? Can you welcome whatever this moment brings?

[5 seconds pause]

Breathing into the left lower leg and as you breathe out inviting the left lower leg to soften and shifting the attention to the left knee. Joints are often carrier that when they work well we barely notice, when they work less slow, there are many emotions that often arise, frustration, and anger. So it's your experience right now.

[5 seconds pause]

At this point you notice the attention drifts away into thoughts or reactions. Noticing wherever it's gone, noticing this is normal this is how the human brain works. Be aware of this noticing is a moment of mindfulness. And chance to invite the attention back to the left knee and all the sensations or lack of sensation is present. Allow the breath to be in left knee and then let it go. Shifting the attention to the left upper leg, thigh, and large muscles on the thigh. Breathing in here till left upper leg and when it feels right inviting it to soften, to release and to let go.

[5 seconds pause]

And then bring the attention to the left hip, so what's here to notice in left hip could be possible to find curiosity for the experience now on the left hip. As if you have never notice to pay attention to the left hip before. Allowing the breath flow to flow in to the left hip and letting go.

[5 seconds pause]

Moving the attention to the ground be aware of whatever there is to feel here in the growing, and the attention to the right hip. Any difference between the right and left hip. Allowing the attention to expand include the whole pelvis. Massive sensations, relax them up and breathing in to the ball of the pelvis. Breathing out and letting go.

[5 seconds pause]

And the travelling with the attention all the way down the right, into the right foot to the right big toe. Beware of anything that arises the attention shifts the right big toe, reactions, thoughts, and emotions. There is no right experience. This is like a exercise in becoming aware of its present.

[5 seconds pause]

So what's there in right big toe, which you might notice? And how about the pink toe and all the toes in between. And then breathing in to all the way don to the toes of the right foot. And as you breathe out letting go.

[5 seconds pause]

Shift the attention to the sole of the right foot. And noticing what's here in the sole of the right foot. Is there tingling or pulsing or perhaps warmth or cold. And breathing in to the sole of the right foot? Release and let go. Bring the attention or the spotlight at the top of the right foot, as if the top of the right foot is your frond and you are quiet curious wanting to know how it's doing. And then allowing the breath to flow to the top of the right foot and as the breath moves out, letting go.

[5 seconds pause]

Shift the attention to the heel of the right foot and then the ankle. Allowing the attention to expand include the whole right foot. Open attention in the whole of right foot. Breathing into the right foot and letting go.

[5 seconds pause]

Shifting the attention to the lower right leg. The calf , the shin , and the bone in the middle. The whole lower right leg, The object of your attention. So what you notice , sometimes you might notice many things and the next time you might notice completely different. So what you notice today and then breathing into the right lower leg and let go as you breathe out. and then guiding the attention to right knee. Noticing what's here. Inviting the breath to flow in, letting go.

[5 seconds pause]

Shift the attention to the upper leg; its muscles, the top and the bottom. Perhaps there is tension in this leg, in these muscles at this moment, perhaps not. Either way is ok and you can breathe in inviting the breath into the upper right leg and breathe out, letting go.

[5 seconds pause]

Shift the attention into the right hip, back to the whole pelvis and then to the back spine. Allow the attention to run through the whole length to the spine up to bottom and bottom to top. What can you notice there, all the little muscles around the spine. Broadening the attention to include the whole surface of the back lower back middle back, the upper back, the right shoulder and the left. This can be a sensitive area; the area prone to tension or soreness. What you notice here in whole surface in the back?

And you might notice how the breath moves in around the spine as you inhale. Like notice how the lungs expand, the side of the ribcage moving out and back in. Wave the sensations of breathing and allowing the attention to roam in the body, the chest, the right and left side of the chest, the center of the chest. Perhaps noticing its rise and fall with the breath. You may also become aware of the heart, beating inside of the chest. Pumping bloods with the whole body. Taking oxygen to lungs and circulating it. Cleaning out the waste and allowing it to exhale. You might breathe in to the whole chest area. Filling it and inviting it to soften as the breath flows out.

[5 seconds pause]

Letting go and allow your attention in to move into the whole belly region and all in this region, the intestine, kidneys, liver, and gallbladder. Imagine as you breathe in how the breath moves in between the organs. As you breathe out letting go, inviting a sense of softness into this place. Allowing the attention to move upwards, from the belly region up to the chest and into the shoulders and down both arms, all the way down into the hands, and thumbs ,the left and the right, right and the left. The index fingers, the middle fingers, the ring fingers and the pinky fingers. What do you notice? What sensations are present what experience now in the fingers of both hands? Allow the attention then to encompass in whole of both hands. Breathing in, releasing, and letting go.

[5 seconds pause]

Shift the attention now to both wrists. Feel the posing are running through the wrists or something else. Whatever the experience is just fine. If you choose you might welcome it. Include any thoughts or emotions or reactions that might arise. Breathe in and let go. Now bring attention to the lower arms. Both lower arms, both elbows and both upper arms. Invite the breath to flow into the arms and the hands, release and let go.

[5 seconds pause]

Choose to place the attention into the throat, into the neck. You can hear the muscles on the throat and feel any tension, sensation, seeing of arteries, feeling this area the neck and the throat and letting go.

[5 seconds pause]

Move the attention into the back of the head. May be there is pressure on the back of the head. And allow the attention to move towards the right ear and the left ear, and both cheeks, the chin, jaw, aware of the muscle in the jaw. They place often tension, anger, frustration. Imagine the breath fills in the muscle of the jaw as the breath flows out inviting them gently to let go.

[5 seconds pause]

Attention inside the mouth, the tongue, the roof of the mouth, the lower lip, the upper lip, the tip of the nose, whole nose and the both eyes. Aware of sensations of any tension of the experience of this moment and right eyebrow and left eyebrow and the space between the eyebrows, forehead, what feelings are on the forehead and then letting go, letting the muscles to soften.

[5 seconds pause]

You might notice that how the breath moves from the crown of the head all the way down to the toes. As you breathe out it moves from the toes to the top of the crown. Breathing in through the crown of the head, all the way down to the toes and out up from the toes all up to the crown of the head, moving in a wave through the body.

[5 minutes pause]

Now, I want you to visualize yourself standing in front of you as if looking into a big mirror. This refection of you that you see in the mirror is your ideal future self that does not smoke. So look clearly. How would the non-smoker you look like? How do you look? How do you feel? Do you look healthier? Do you look a bit younger? Is your skin more vibrant now? And what about your face? Do you look happier now? Can you see the sparkle in your eyes? Do you appear to be more at peace? Can you notice your body language? Do you appear more confident? Do you seem more energetic? Can you sense your self-esteem?

[5 seconds pause]

Take your time and look in detail how exactly would you look and feel if you had quit smoking forever?

[30 seconds pause]

In front of you is the version of you that doesn't smoke. Your non-smoker self has all the qualities of a non-smoker but is not missing out the benefits you associate with cigarettes. You can see the non-smoker you in the mirror to be more relaxed, more comfortable, and more confident. All the qualities that you aspire are already there in your non-smoker self. The health benefits, self-control, confidence, peace of mind, balanced emotions, clarity of thoughts. You can see how happy you are. How much more control you seem to have over your life.

[5 seconds pause]

Now I want you to float into that ideal non-smoking self. See from the eyes and hear from the ears of that non-smoker you. Feel the feelings.

[5 seconds pause]

Feel it in your mind, feel it in your body, and feel it in your senses – the relief and good feelings you get as a non-smoker. Everything looks brighter and bigger. Everything feels so much better. You feel so healthy. The air feels so fresh and pure. And your lungs – your lungs feel so clean and cleansed. They breathe perfectly. Feel how fresh and new the air feels now with these smoke-free lungs. Feel how sufficient and powerful your lungs feel now. And you feel so good about yourself. You have never felt happier. You have never felt so good. It's just fantastic! You feel empowered. There's an extraordinary confidence within you. You feel you could anything, you could be anything. And your health is at its ideal best now. You look so fit and so good. You feel so good from the inside. All your cells, all your organs have been cleansed of the harmful chemicals and tar and nicotine. You can finally feel the health resonating within you. You are healthy, you are nourished. And from the outside, you look great. Your eyes are sparkling with a new confidence. Your skin is shining and vibrant. You are at your perfect weight and size. Everything about you is just perfect. And you are enjoying every moment of this new life. What more changes do you see in your ideal non-smoker self?

[5 minutes]

Now, I will be counting from one to ten. And when I reach ten, I want you to open your eyes and be fully aware. This is to bring you back from the state of hypnosis to the state of normal alertness. With each number I say, you will become more and more relaxed and more and more aware of yourself and your surroundings.

So, starting with One. You are back in your consciousness.

Two. Become more alert.

Three. Feeling your body

Four. Feeling your emotions.

Five. Listening to the sounds outside.

Six. Becoming aware of your sense of smell.

Seven. Feeling the texture of clothing on your skin.

Eight. You are back in your body.

Nine. You are aware. You are in the present moment.

Ten. Gently open your eyes. Welcome Back!

2. Quit Smoking Hypnosis – II (60 minutes)

This is a quit smoking hypnosis audio. Do not listen to this recording when you are operating heavy machinery. You should preferably be lying down or sitting comfortably on your bed, sofa, or a mat. This hypnosis should best be enjoyed using headphones. By the time you reach the end of this audio, you will wake up completely relaxed and reinvigorated.

So, close your eyes and listen to my voice with full focus and follow my instructions. If your mind wanders during the course of the hypnosis, gently bring it back. Right now, you need to simply relax and let go of any thoughts. Loosen up your body. First I will be relaxing your physical body to make it easier for your subconscious mind to follow my instructions and act on it. So, let's begin.

Inhale through the nose and exhale through the mouth. Breathing in deeply through the belly, up to your chest and as you exhale allow your body to relax.

[5 seconds pause]

You can imagine yourself with each in breath that you breathing in life force energy. In your every exhale which you releasing, stress and dense energy stuck in your body. Take three deep breaths in and out together and make sure when exhale is a little longer than inhale and also allows to your resistance to relax.

Take deep inhale and then a slow exhale. Deep inhale and slow exhale. As you deeper in and exhale. Continue to breathe deeply on your own pace breathing into the nose and out through the mouth.

[5 seconds pause]

While breathing you can become aware of how your body feels. And know that there is no right and wrong to feel. Just allow yourself to become aware of any sensations in your body. It might also be some tension or some heaviness. Just allow yourself to become aware of it without necessarily efforts to change it. Just notice where your awareness you can slowly get to through entering your body.

[5 seconds pause]

Now again use your awareness to scan every part of your body. We going to start all the way down to your feet, to your toes, if you want, you can move your feet and your toes, to feel the ground beneath you. Let go of any thoughts and relax completely. Allow your toes, your feet to relax a little bit more, to become aware of any tension.

[5 seconds pause]

Now move up the ankles, up to your calves, your shims, to your knees. With each inhale we are going to breathe in life force energy. With each exhale we are going to release, let go, little bit more of a tension that heaviness. Allow all the stuck energy to free up.

[5 seconds pause]

There are going to move up to thighs, hips, and often we load lot of tensions in our hips. It is also ok to move your hips a little bit. You can move them side ways, back and forth even in a spiral motion. Becoming aware of any tension that is ready to be released. Again there is no right and wrong way to feel. Now you can allow the movement to gently and naturally to come again to a still point. You can allow it to slowly and naturally to come back to its center again.

[5 seconds pause]

Now we are going up to your belly. Becoming aware of any emotions to be there, or any other sensations. You can just breathe through it. Allowing yourself to breathe deeply to that area. Making sure you can breathe deeply and slowly there is no need to rush. Through your belly your body is going to relax. Let go of any thoughts and relax completely. When you are ready you can move up little bit more. Become aware of the middle back, upper abdomen. And with every exhale you can allow that breath to release and move back. Inhale and exhale in your own pace. Allow yourself to sink deeper in your body, allow yourself to go deeper into the state of relaxation.

[5 seconds pause]

We are continuing to move up with your awareness. Move on to your upper back, inner chest. Become aware of the front and the back of the heart space; any emotions and sensations that beside in that heart space. In that space of feeling sensation and emotions are welcome to be loved. Know that is safe here. And further parts still feels anxious or hurt or stress or fatigue it's safe to relax now. If any of part is not ready to relax, know that's completely fine too. We can just invite them to be in the warmth of heart space.

[5 seconds pause]

Now become aware of your shoulders. Allow those muscles to loosen up, breathing through that area. Let go of tension. You can repeat this few times. With every in breath, breathing in and receiving more energy. With every out breath, letting go little bit more of any tension, any stress, any wave which we still carrying and ready to let go up. Allowing the breaths to guide you, allow your body to move. Whatever way you want to and wish to release that energy. Let go of any thoughts and relax completely.

[5 seconds pause]

Now become aware of your arms. Allow your awareness to move down to your hands, fingertips. Allow your hands to relax more deeply. You can allow your energy to up again. Up to your neck and also in neck we hold lot of tension. So you can allow your head to roll, your neck to move .allowing your neck to move in whatever way, you wants to move. Bring your awareness to your head now. Allow those muscles to relax softly. With your breath you can continue to release any tension that is still there.

[5 seconds pause]

Now go up to the face, starting with your jaw. Allowing your jaw to relax and mouth to open. We can even stretch our jaw with our mouth wide open. Allow your jaw to drop so that no longer holding on to the tension, allowing that jaw to drop completely. Allow that tension to release. When we tend to control our stress we get really tend to anxious in that area. So while breathing in through the nose and out through the mouth, feel so relax. And now we allow that relaxation to spread all over face.

[5 seconds pause]

Allow our nose muscles to relax, ears, cheeks, eyes, eyebrows, forehead. Now allowing that relaxation to move all the way over your scalp, the crown of the head over the back to the neck. Continuing to breathe that relaxation. Letting go of the tension. With each inhale, breathing in deeper relaxation and with each exhale letting go little bit more. Let go of any thoughts and relax completely.

[5 seconds pause]

Continue to breathing deeply through the belly. Now can make them aware part of your body you are feeling the most tension or stress. And now focus on that area specifically. To brief through that area. In it with your breath, you can soften those muscles, soften that area. Allowing the tension to release and to move out or being gently transformed by breath. Without forcing anything here, you are just inviting and allowing anything that needs to let go, be released. You can continue to soften any area you still feeling stress. Let go of any thoughts and relax completely. Again breathing in to your nose and out through your mouth. Allowing your jaws relax and all the energies in your body able to move freely.

[5 seconds pause]

Continue to soften the muscles with the breaths. Allow all parts of your body to relax. Let go of any thoughts and relax completely. Allow your body to sink deeper into the ground. To come to the earth to be rooted in gently you can also send back nay energy that you don't need, any tension back to the earth all the way down with your feet, with of course with the permission of mother earth. Allow her to receive it fully.

[5 seconds pause]

Know that your body is beautiful expression, creation of nature. Continue to soften your body. Allow it to relax more deeply that you are safe here in this moment. Take a moment to call back all your energy back into your body to go back all your awareness back in to your sacred temple. You can visualize lotus opening up softly. Allow all your energies to come back fully in your body. Allow that energy to move all the way down, breathing that energy in all parts of your body. That's a place where you want to be right now, here in this moment, fully embodied, energetic opening in a crown. You can also bring in light golden energy from the sun, from the heaven and bring it all the way down, allowing that life force energy to fuel you. Let go of any thoughts and relax completely. Breathe that energy in, let that energy spread your body, merging with the energy of mother earth, lighting up any heaviness.

[5 seconds pause]

Feel the empty space and all the corners from your body from your head all the way down your toes. Allow your body to energies and soak up that white golden light. Let go of any thoughts and relax completely. Now allow yourself to breathe deeply in a circular motion. Inhale and the exhale in a single continuous motion so that you are not stopping the breath in between. Allowing all your energy in your body, in your breath to move and flow freely. Allow yourself to receive the energy of the mother earth, of the sun, of the solar. We can fully energies our body and just receive for moment. Let go of any thoughts and relax completely. Continue to breathe deeply in your own pace. Now hold that energy to ground deeply in your body. Now take three breaths together. Taking a deep breath in and then exhaling. Allow yourself to release any energy that we want to release and you can also allow to release any energy out through your mouth open. You can even make a sound, really open up a jaw to release. Take a deep breath in, filling up the belly and out. Now breathe at your normal relaxed pace.

[30 seconds]

Welcome a bright blue light coming to you. And only with in-breath, we are going to allow this bright blue nourishing light to come in with our breath into our bodies. So we are going to breathe in, feeling its warmth comes in through our mouth and out from our nose. And it's going to go above neck to up on our spine and into our brain. So still breathing in and feeling that bright blue light coming to us and entering into our heads like a light ball. Nourishing and untangling our addiction to smoking. Just allow that bright blue light as we breathe in to calm, sooth all those pulses in our brains, in our control center; still breathing in this bright blue light. And feeling that pressure release and drop inside your head, to your thoughts and desires quiet and sooth and clam. Still breathing in that bright blue light to your head and your brain and allowing it to reset all of those connections. And as this happens and as this a way, this bright blue light and calmness in your brain is sent for to communicate with all the rest in your body.

[5 seconds pause]

So as you breathe in this bright blue light into your brain all that messages of calm and peace, set down your spine and shoulders in your back, in your hands, in your palms and fingers. To your neck and your chest, to your stomach, to your hips and your thighs and your knees, your legs and your ankles, your toes. Let go of any thoughts and relax completely. Feel it calmly and gently restoring you, giving peace. Knowing and feeling that you all need right now to feel this feeling.

[5 seconds pause]

So as we breathe this bright blue light in, to our brains. Allow it to flow all of this messages, communications to the rest of our bodies feeling nice and calm. Bring your attention to the out breath. So as we breathe in that bright blue light is coming in and nourishing us. And now as we breathe out, just take all of that resistance, that tension, that longing, that energy pace of addiction to be released as a thick dark smoke and mist that will leave you and go back into the universe, back to the soil of its own natural state to nourish the earth.

[5 seconds pause]

So breathing in, that bright blue light that nourishes and breathing out and releasing that tension and stickiness. Setting up a Cycle with inner selves, breathingin, back what nourishes us, resets us and breathing out to releasing that which doesn't serve us and needs to leave. Breathing in and breathing out.

[5 seconds pause]

Now just send the ball and just know that you are protected, loved, and able to do this now for yourself just for few minutes.

[5 minutes pause]

Just continuing to breathe in bright blue light and release that smoke or fog when you breathe out.so it is important to remember that all we are doing here is helping the body, the mind and the soul, reset and remember your natural state.

[5 seconds pause]

Each moment in your road to recovering remember that. That you are simply shedding things which are wild and taken on. And it requires work and efforts. It is simply taking layer of not acquiring a new mindset or a new logic. Reminding and remembering your body, your mind and your soul that your natural state is one of health, abundance and love. Before we end, just give thanks to yourself. It is so important what you not just for you, not just for your loved ones but to the earth and every being on it.

[30 seconds pause]

It's now time to come back to your awareness. I will be counting very slowly from five to zero. You also need not hurry. Follow my instructions as I guide you back home. You will be becoming more aware with each receding number, and become fully aware when I reach the number zero.

Five. You are here in the present moment now. Be in the here. Be in the now. Bring your consciousness back to your body. Slowly begin to realize that you are in your physical body. Slowly and gently come back to the present moment.

Four. Feel your body. Feel your feet, your legs, and your hips. Feel your abdomen and your chest region. Feel your entire spinal column, feel your back. Be aware of your hands and wrists and your elbows and your entire arms. Now your shoulders and neck and chin. Now bring your awareness into your entire face. Feel your eyes resting in your sockets; now your forehead and your scalp. In a moment, be aware of your entire physical body.

Three. Clench your fists. And release. Move your fingers and toes. Loosen up your shoulders. Rotate your ankles, knees. Relax your jaw.

Two. Feel the flow of energy. Be in the present moment. Feel your breath. Feel the sensations.

One. Be aware of the surroundings. Can you hear any sound coming from outside the room? Can you smell anything? Can you feel the textures of your clothing?

Zero. When you are ready, gently open your eyes. Welcome back!

3. Quit Smoking Hypnosis – III (70 minutes)

You are listening to this audio because you have decided to quit smoking. You are about to get into a hypnotic trance; so do not listen to this audio while you are driving or doing something that requires your attention. You should preferably be lying down or sitting comfortably on your bed, sofa, or a mat. This hypnosis should best be enjoyed using headphones. By the time you reach the end of this audio, you will wake up completely relaxed and reinvigorated.

You may or may not notice any changes in your body during this hypnosis. It is quite normal to fall asleep. It won't matter if you snooze off listening to this audio because your subconscious mind would still be alert and listening to my instructions. So, close your eyes and let go of any thoughts that have been troubling you. This time is solely for your healing. Listen to my voice with full focus and follow my instructions. If your mind wanders during the course of the hypnosis, gently bring it back. Right now, you need to simply relax and let go of any thoughts. Loosen up your body. First I will be relaxing your physical body to make it easier for your subconscious mind to follow my instructions and act on it. So, let's begin with some breathing. Try to breathe as deeply as possible while maintaining a gentle focus on the movement of the breath.

[5 seconds pause]

Breathe in and breathe out. Breathe in and out.

[5 seconds pause]

In and out.

[20 seconds pause]

We are going to be scanning the body. From the feet all the way up to the head. As we do this we will be dancing and relaxing muscle groups. Whenever you are ready bring all your awareness down to the feet now. Become aware of the toes, the soles of the feet, the heels. On your next inhale you are going to lift your legs in inch of the mat or the bed and tense your feet. So breathe in tense the feet, and exhale the feet. Relax the toes, relax the feet, relax the heels and ankles, relax. Now bring your awareness to the legs, notice the shins, calves, knees, thighs, ham strings.

[5 seconds pause]

On your next inhale you are going to lift your legs. On your next inhale, you are going to lift the legs again, breathe in let the legs and in tense the legs, intense and exhale drop the legs. Relax the legs, relax the shins, cleaves, relax the knees, thighs, relax the hamstrings, feel completely relaxed.

[5 seconds pause]

Now bring your awareness to your hips. Notice the pelvis, the gluteus on your next inhale you are going to slightly lift your pelvis and tense the gluteus. Breathe in and tense the gluteus, tense and exhale, release and relax. Relaxing the pelvis, relaxing the hips, relax. Now bring your awareness to your abdomen. Become aware of internal organs, the gut, many people consider the gut to be the second mind. It affects so much of our mental wellbeing. So give yourself this opportunity to have the intentions to release toxins from the gut. On your next inhale you will tense the abdominal muscle. Breathe in to the belly and tense the abdominal muscle and exhale. You even want to take another deep breath in. take a deep breath into the belly and relax. Relaxing the abdominal muscles, relaxing the gut, relax.

[5 seconds pause]

Now bring your awareness to your chest. Become aware of the heart, the heart-center and the lungs. This is where we feel emotions such as compassion, joy, and peace. This is also where we feel sadness, loneliness and pain. So give yourself this opportunity to release any repressed emotions or energies from this area. Take a deep breath in and tensing a rib cage, tense, tense and exhale. Relaxing the chest, relaxing the heart and the lungs, relax. You even want to a another breath in, fill the lungs up and breath out completely.

[5 seconds pause]

I want you to bring your awareness to your shoulders now. This is very attentive for you, burden and stress. Be unconsciously tense our shoulders without even realizing it. You have this opportunity now to release all tension from the shoulders. On your next inhale shrugs your shoulders at your ears and tense, tense, and exhale of the shoulder. Creating space between the ears and the shoulders lengthen the neck. You may even want to rotate the neck from side to side, create space and release tension. When you are ready you can return to the center and realign the spine. Relaxing the shoulders, relaxing the neck, releasing tension and stress, release and relax.

[5 seconds pause]

Now bring your awareness to your arms, notice the hands and fingers also. We tend to feel emotions such as frustration and anger in our hands and so give yourself opportunity to release any frustration or anger. On your next inhale you are going to lift your arms, breathe in lifting your arms slightly make fists with both hands and now spread the fingers out wide, tense and exhale drop the arms , relax hands and fingers. Relaxing the arms, relaxing the hands, relaxing the fingers. Releasing repressed energy, relax.

[5 seconds pause]

Now bring your awareness to your face. We make thousands of expressions in the face. Many of us like to keep a poker face throughout the day. Therefore repressing emotions. This is your opportunity to release repressed emotions and refresh this emotional slate. Take a deep breathe in and tense the facial muscles and crushed the face towards the nose make an ugly frown and exhale. Completely relax the face. Creating space between the eyebrows and forehead, creating space all around the eyes and around the nose. Allow your lips to part, and relax the tongue. loosen the jaw allow it to hang those. Relax the throat, ears and even scalp, relax. At this point you have relax your entire body from the tip of your toes all the way up to the top of the head. You have relax your entire body from the top of the head all the way down to the tip of the toes. You are relaxed, you are relaxed.

[5 seconds pause]

Allow your body to get heavy, your limbs are length and loose. You are going to mentally repeat after me. My feet are relaxed, my legs are relaxed, my pelvis is relaxed, my belly is relaxed, my chest is relaxed, my shoulders are relaxed. My arms are relaxed, my hand are relaxed, my face is relaxed, my body is relaxed, my mind is relaxed, I am relaxed. Your whole is relaxed. Your mind is relaxed. You are completely at peace.

[30 seconds pause]

I want you to imagine a time in future, may be a year from today, and visualise yourself as a non-smoker. It's been one year since you smoked your last cigarette and you feel so good about making and keeping that decision. Your life has changed entirely, and you feel so good about it now. You can recall how you used to doubt if you could ever quit smoking and here you are now having gone through a full year without smoking a single puff. And that's an achievement. And you know you can continue this good habit forever. Because it wasn't as bad as you thought it would be. Once you made that decision to quit smoking, you kept it. And you can clearly see the results. You are now so much happier and healthier than you were a year before. This one year as a non-smoker has given you tremendous benefits. You are now so much fitter than before. You are now so much in control of your thoughts and emotions. You are now in charge of your life. Until a year ago you couldn't resist the temptation to smoke. But now you can walk past the smokers with ease and grace and polite reject their offer to smoke with them. And that confidence that you have gained in the past twelve months is remarkable. It shows on your face, the way you walk, how you talk to others. It's simply impressive to say the least. And you are enjoying every moment of this new healthy life. And you wonder if this one year has been so much remarkable how great the rest of your life would become as a non-smoker.

[5 seconds pause]

As a non-smoker, you are now living the life you knew you were meant for. The decision to quit smoking forever has had such a positive spill over effect on your life. And you see it as a blessing. Your life is now so much better. You can now see how much good things were missing from your life when you used to smoke. But now, one year after your decision to quit smoking, life seems to be so much pleasant. Everything in your life has changed for the better. Your health is at its peak. On fitness front, you are at your ideal weight and size. And people around you can't help but shower compliments and praises upon you. Your transformation truly has been inspiring. Your life as a non-smoker, one year down the line, has open up gates of great opportunities and fortune. And you are embracing all the good things in life. And you can notice how you have become a magnet that attracts abundance and prosperity. Everything that you need in life to grow and prosper is finding its way to you. And you wonder if all of this has something to do with your decision to quit smoking? And the answer is yes, absolutely! Because when you make changes in your life for the betterment of your health and future, the universe conspires to reward you for commitment to positive change.

[5 seconds pause]

And the best thing about the non-smoker you is that you are not missing out on any benefits you used to associate with smoking. You can recall how you used smoking to control your emotions or to cope with stress. And you had this wrong belief that you need to continue smoking to manage stress. But now you realise that cigarettes had nothing to do with controlling emotions and anxiety. It was your internal response mechanism that responded to the stimulus of smoking to release chemicals that made you feel better. Today, as a non-smoker, your body's composition has not changed, but the stimulus has. The same chemicals that were secreted when you smoked a cigarette are now secreted naturally without any requirement for you to smoke. Now, whenever you feel the craving to smoke, you just take three deep and long breaths, and your body responds to the stimulus and secretes chemicals that make you feel relaxed. And the more you practice this habit, the more in-control you become. You can now notice that the cravings have become minimal. You rarely feel the craving to smoke. It's been one year you have quit smoking and you have decided to quit smoking forever.

Even as a non-smoker you continue to enjoy the good feelings you once associated with cigarettes. And now you are also enjoying the benefits of good health. And when I say health, your subconscious mind automatically understands that I am talking about both physical and mental health. Your subconscious mind will find ways to get rid of the unhealthy habits and effects of smoking but keep the good feelings you associate with cigarettes. Your subconscious mind will work in a way that you enjoy the best of both the worlds. Now you will never again smoke a cigarette in life yet continue to keep the good effects of smoking. You will be a non-smoker for the rest of your life and yet keep with you all the good things you enjoyed because of your old habits. Your body will automatically adjust to help you manage your emotions. You will be in complete control of yourself. And you won't have to do any extra efforts for that because your subconscious mind knows how to make adjustments to keep the good effects of old habits. Your inner systems will be rewired to help you keep the rewards of smoking but the good thing is that you won't feel the need to smoke. You will never again smoke and still enjoy the good feelings you once associated with smoking. That's exactly what your subconscious mind is being programmed for right now. it will readjust all the inner mechanisms of your body to make sure you adapt to the new smoke-free life effortlessly and smoothly. And you don't even need to know how that will happen because change that stays is always organic and natural. Your transition into a non-smoker will happen naturally. You will leave behind your old habits and lead a life of a healthy, happy, and energetic you. And these subtle changes are happening in the background as you listen to this audio.

[5 seconds pause]

And don't worry about how is this happening or if it will work for you. Things that happen naturally usually work without your knowledge. The growth of a tree is natural and so will be your growth into a healthier version of you. And that change will make you strong and confident. Imagine how good you would feel without the craving to smoke in future. How confident you would be in public. The self-restraint will give so much confidence to you. And the self-discipline will develop naturally as the time passes. Your subconscious mind can take as much it needs to make this possible. Your change that is natural takes its own time. And when such a change happens it happens fundamentally. It doesn't target the symptoms. It will target the main reasons as to why you smoke and heal that cause so that you will never again in your life feel the urge to pick up a cigarette.

[5 seconds pause]

Your subconscious mind is so strong that when it follows a command and takes actions to achieve the goal it won't stop until the mission is achieved. Your life is full of examples when your subconscious mind made a strong decision and stuck to it. If you can think of a time when you made a decision and took actions to achieve that goal and finally reached your mark, I want you to feel that feeling of accomplishment now. Whether you know or not your subconscious mind has a big role to play in making you stick to your goals. It keeps you charged and gives you the strength whenever you feel weak. And this time your subconscious mind is being programmed in such a way that it will find ways to make you a non-smoker. The changes in your body at the cellular level are already happening. Your subconscious mind is affecting changes in your physiology to make you a permanent non-smoker. And you need not know how it will happen because change will happen naturally and organically.

And change that is happening now will be fun. You will enjoy your transition into a non-smoker. You will not feel forced to do any tasks. But why would you smoke when there is no craving and no need to do so? Your subconscious mind is being programmed in such a way that it will make the transition fun. You won't notice how the changes happened because they will happen naturally. And at the end of it all you will be the happiest, healthiest, and best version of yourself.

And the change is already happening. From this moment on, you have embarked on a journey to a smoke-free you. You have made a decision to choose health over diseases and freedom over dependency. You have decided to breathe the fresh air and enjoy the little joys of life. And each day from this day, you will become healthier and happier. You have made the decision to quit smoking because your health is important to you. From now on, you will be completely active and alert and vigilant. You are no longer a slave of cigarettes. You made a decision to quit smoking and you successfully stuck by that decision.

[10 seconds pause]

And now as a non-smoker you are enjoying your life to the fullest. There's no looking back. Every night you sleep without any guilt or worry. Every morning you wake up healthy, refreshed, and rejuvenated. You take in three deep breaths and can feel the fresh air entering your body and energising each and every cell in your body. It feels so great to start your day like this. You have this feeling that there's so much in store for you. And you are genuinely happy for this new life as a non-smoker. There's no craving. You are in complete control. And you also notice that your productivity at work has increased manifold. Your focus has multiplied. Your output has increased manifold. And you wonder to yourself if this all the result of your decision to quit smoking? And the answer is yes, absolutely! The smoke-free life has improved your productivity. Your health is at its optimum best. Your lungs work perfectly. You feel so good about your health now. And everyone can notice that now you are much more calm than before. You are in control of your life. You have clarity.

And you can visualise yourself in that calmness and control. Visualise a confident you that does not smoke at all. This new you is full of all the qualities that you aspire for. See that charismatic personality that is full of health and confidence. See the non-smoker version of you as clearly as possible.

[5 seconds pause]

Now float into that self-image. See through your eyes of the non-smoker you. Feel the confidence, the charisma. Feel that good feeling of health and fitness. Now feel how relaxed and in control it feels to be a non-smoker. Stay in that zone of comfort and ease. Let your subconscious mind soak in that perfect-self image.

[5 seconds pause]

Visualise yourself in a gathering among your friends. Visualise the non-smoker you who is confident and calm and is full of charm and charisma. You are happily socialising with people around you, and when someone offers you a cigarette, you confidently look into their eyes and politely reply, "No, thank you, I don't smoke." And they can see the sparkle in your eyes. Your demeanour is so impressive. You are enjoying your freedom as a non-smoker. Let your subconscious mind have a clear self-image of the non-smoker you. And it doesn't matter if you remember this image later or not because once your subconscious mind captures something, that image is stored in it for ever.

[5 smoker]

Live the life of a non-smoker. Feel how good it feels to breathe in the fresh air every time you inhale. Feel the control that you now have over your life. Free from all cravings and addictions. And whenever there is even the slightest of urge, you just take three deep and long breaths. And you can feel that craving going away. And it feels so good to have full control over your emotions. You have got your technique and it works every single time. And this gives you so much confidence. You are able to do this because you honour and respect your health and wellbeing. You know how important it is to stay healthy. Your healthy lungs are a reminder how much it means to you to be a non-smoker. And you feel the gratitude deep in your heart.

[10 seconds pause]

The technique is working wonders for you now. You now know that whenever there is even the slightest of craving, you have to take three deep and long breaths and the craving will vanish. And you wonder why even wait for the craving to arise, I will make this my habit to take three deep and long breaths whenever I want to feel good about myself. And you will notice that this will work every single time. So, the next time you feel stressed, just take three deep and long breaths and the stress will disappear. Not just stress but any type of obstacle you face in your life you can use this technique to balance yourself and fill your mind and body with positive energy. You will be so much more in control of your mind and emotions. No emotion will now be able to overwhelm you. You are in charge. You are in control. Whenever a challenge arises, you repeat this breathing technique and feel a sense of calm and balance fill your body and mind. Visualise yourself overcoming any challenges or obstacles that may come across your path. Feel yourself standing your ground with calm and confidence and coming out victorious. Feel that feeling.

[5 seconds pause]

And the same goes for any urge for smoking you may ever feel, the breathing technique will give you strength and clarity. Once you have won over your mind, you can win over anything. Your subconscious mind has been programmed in such a way that no insecurity, so craving can ever touch you. Your subconscious mind will alert you to practice this technique to overcome any hurdles that may come across your life as a non-smoker. Whatever you listened to today, you need not remember. But you must return to it time and again. You must listen to this recording every day for at least twenty-one days to let the message seep into your psyche. Because the change we are aiming for today is a life-long change. Your life will change completely and for the good. You will be leading a healthy and prosperous life. Your subconscious mind is being trained to open avenues to make that happen. And soon you will see opportunities coming your way and resources showing up unexpectedly. But everything will happen at the right time. And when that time comes, you must be ready. That is why it is imperative that you listen to this recording for twenty-one days. A reminder has been set in your sub-conscious mind. You will be alert and vigilant from now on to opportunities and avenues that will lead you to the life of a successful non-smoker. Pay heed to those nudges.

[5 seconds pause]

Your subconscious mind knows what's good for you. It knows how to turn you into a non-smoker. Your subconscious mind has patiently listened to all my commands. It doesn't matter if your conscious mind wandered away during the hypnosis. This hypnosis wasn't meant for your conscious mind. Your subconscious mind has received the commands. Whether you feel it or not but your metabolism has already sprung into action. Your body is preparing for the life of a non-smoker. You are about to quit smoking forever. This is the first step towards the life as a non-smoker. Your subconscious mind will now find ways to activate the commands it received today. And it will do so in such a way that you don't miss out on the good feelings you associate with smoking. So, you will have the best of both the worlds. You will be a non-smoker and at the same time will enjoy the good feelings and control over your emotions. Your subconscious mind will take the necessary steps to achieve that goal.

[30 seconds pause]

Now, I will be counting from one to ten. And when I reach ten, I want you to open your eyes and be fully aware. This is to bring you back from the state of hypnosis to the state of normal alertness. With each number I say, you will become more and more relaxed and more and more aware of yourself and your surroundings.

One. You are conscious of your existence.

Two. You can listen to your mind's chatter.

Three. You are aware of the temperature of the room you are in.

Four. Feeling the clothing on your skin.

Five. Engaging the sense of smell.

Six. What noises can you listen to?

Seven. You are back in your sense, back in your awareness.

Eight. You are aware of the present moment, aware of your breathing.

Nine. You can feel your body. You know exactly where you are now.

Ten. Coming back completely into the physical awareness, feel your presence, feel your being. Gently open your eyes. Welcome Back!

4. Quit Smoking Hypnosis - IV (70 minutes)

Do not listen to this audio when you are driving or doing something that requires your attention. You should preferably be lying down or sitting comfortably on your bed, sofa, or a mat. This hypnosis should best be enjoyed using headphones. By the time you reach the end of this audio, you will wake up completely relaxed and reinvigorated.

So, close your eyes and let go of any thoughts that have been troubling you. This time is solely for your healing. Listen to my voice with full focus and follow my instructions. If your mind wanders during the course of the hypnosis, gently bring it back. Right now, you need to simply relax and let go of any thoughts. Loosen up your body. First I will be relaxing your physical body to make it easier for your subconscious mind to follow my instructions and act on it. So, let's begin.

Bring your awareness to your breath. And as you bring your awareness to your breath, you notice that how you are inhaling and exhaling every time you breathe. Inhale your breath deeply now. Hold it and exhale. Let's do it one more time. Inhale deeply from your nose, hold it for a few seconds. And exhale now. Now come to your normal breathing pattern. Feel relaxed and calm with each word I say. Feel a sense of calm envelope you.

[5 seconds pause]

As you allow yourself to relax, shift your focus or awareness to your toes.as you do that stretch out your toes and then simply relax as you bring them back to their normal position. Now tighten your calves muscle, as if you are squeezing them in for a few seconds and them simply let go them as you relax and release. Allowing yourself to relax any discomfort or tightness in your calves. Now tighten thigh muscles , just as you did with your calves muscles. Squeeze them in hold for a few seconds and relax. Breathing calmly.

[5 seconds pause]

Now shift your focus from your legs to the mid-section of your body. You now tense your butt muscle. If you could squeeze them in for a few moments and then relax. Feeling all the relaxation going in to your toes, heels, ankles, clave muscles, thighs and hips. As you continue to breathe slowly, your feel more relaxed.

Now shift your to your upper body, starting with your stomach and back. Bring all your awareness to the lower abdomen, squeezing I the muscles and then releasing them slowly. Letting go any stress and tightness. Now take a deep breath again. Feeling the air going in side of your stomach. And when you exhale you mentally let go of any thoughts or feelings. That may be bothering you lately. Now slowly shift your awareness to your hands. If you could tighten your fists, really hard and hold them for a few moments. And now as you relax you open your fists slowly, letting any tightness or stress, simply fade away.

[5 seconds pause]

Now bring all your awareness to your arms and as you do so, you simply tighten all and every muscle of your arm. As you bring them closer towards your body. holding them like that for a moment. And now relax. You bring all your awareness to your upper body, to your shoulders and back. And as you do so simply lift your shoulders up towards your ears, hold them tight and tightening them. Stay in this position for next 5 seconds. Now release and relax yourself fully. Let your shoulders back to their normal positions. As you do that, all the discomfort that you may have or any stress you feel in your back and shoulders simply fade away.

Now bring your focus to all your facial muscles, perhaps those tiny muscles around your eyes. And as you do that you squeeze your eyes, tightening your eye muscle in holding them like that for a few moments. And you now release. Now you allow your focus to shift to your jaw muscle. Feeling the tension in the jaw and now relax .let your jaw come back to its normal position. Now imagine the colour that represents relaxation or peace to you. Now imagine that colour magically appearing in front of you. It looks beautiful so relaxing, just to look at it. And you touch it may be it's a ball, filled with that colour. That exudes a beautiful energy. As you touch it you notice that energy entering your fingers, your palms , your hands, moving up into your arms , shoulders, back, your neck, moving up into your chin, your lips, your nose , your head. Coming down to your eras, going into your shoulders again. Now touching the centre of your chest and moving down into your stomach, your mid section, your hips, your legs, your calves, and your feet. Imagine this beautiful relaxation, in your entire body, in every cell, fibre, bone, muscle and nerve. Your body is shining with this peaceful energy. So calm and relaxed. Feel the peace all over you. Feel it.

[30 seconds pause]

As you listen to what I am saying, you are getting into deeper and deeper levels of trance. You need not be actively following my instructions because I am not talking to your conscious mind. At this deepest level of trance, your subconscious mind is receiving my messages and is already working on them. Your conscious mind might be wandering away or it might have fallen asleep. It might be making plans for the next day or might be recreating past events. Your conscious mind might find it hard to concentrate on my words. Actually, it need not pay attention. Your conscious mind need not fully comprehend the meaning of what I am saying. Don't force your conscious mind; let it rest. It's your subconscious mind that I am talking to – directly. So, when you listen to what I say, it may mean something to you. Or you may not understand it. But you are here for a reason. You are listening to this audio because you have decided to quit smoking. And this decision was not easy. You might have tried to quit smoking before but failed. Don't worry. You won't fail this time. It's your intention that matters. Your subconscious mind is already grasping my messages. Your subconscious mind is being reprogrammed. Keep in mind that you weren't born with a cigarette in your mouth. You learned how to smoke and made it a habit. And if you can learn something, you can surely unlearn it. Your subconscious mind is being reprogrammed in such a way that it will unlearn the habit of smoking. Then you won't have to do any efforts to become a non-smoker. You will be a non-smoker, a natural non-smoker. So, what matters is your decision to become a non-smoker. You made this decision because you respect and honor yourself. You know that you deserve the freedom that comes by being a non-smoker. You know that as a non-smoker, you can live your life more freely, more actively. You will be the one in charge of your life. You will be free of this habit of smoking. You have realized that being a non-smoker means living a healthy life. You will be much more productive and effective.

[5 seconds pause]

Your subconscious mind is being programmed to live the life as a non-smoker so that you can be free of all the health and mental problems that smoking was causing you but at the same time you will continue to enjoy the good feelings you used to associate with cigarettes. You will have the best of both the worlds. Your subconscious mind now knows that and is being programmed to achieve this goal. From now on, you will strengthen your connection to health and wellbeing. You will be more and in control of your emotions and feelings. Your subconscious mind is making all the adjustments to prepare you for the life as a non-smoker. All your organs and all your cells are making adjustments to help adapt to this decision of being a non-smoker. And all this is happening so smoothly and organically that your conscious mind will never get to know if any changes occurred. But changes are taking place in your body right now. These changes will lead you on path to a smooth transition into the life as a non-smoker. The chemistry of your body is changing. You are becoming more and more alert. The good feelings you associated with smoking a cigarette, you continue to enjoy those feelings but without burning a cigarette.

[5 seconds pause]

You will continue to enjoy and feel the pleasures but you won't feel the need to smoke. You will no longer crave for cigarettes. You will lead a healthy, smoke-free life. And life will be so much better on all accounts. You will be so much confident in public spaces. You will be calm and confident and at your charismatic best. And the best thing is that you can confidently say "No, thank you, I don't smoke" when someone offers you a cigarette. And the look on your face, that confidence that is so natural, no one can force you to smoke anymore. And you will still enjoy all the benefits. The good feelings that you associate with smoking, you will still enjoy those feelings but without burning a cigarette. That's how your subconscious mind is being programmed. You will take in just the benefits and no harms. And your life will be so good, so perfect.

[5 seconds pause]

Now you are living the life of a non-smoker. You can feel the freedom that comes by being a non-smoker. You now know what it means to be free, to be in charge of your life. You are the captain of your own ship. No longer are you a slave to those unhealthy and poisonous cigarettes. You feel so healthy – healthy from within. You are full of energy and vitality. You now live this life of complete freedom, complete control, and full of energy. You now see yourself going about your day as a non-smoker. You wake up with the freedom of not feeling the craving to smoke. So you wake and you sit down and you take three deep breaths. This is how you start your day – by taking long and deep breaths, filling your lungs completely. And it all feels so good. You enjoy each breath as you inhale the fresh air, hold it in your lungs for a moment and then exhale fully. It feels so pleasant. You have never felt so alive before. Every breath you take as a non-smoker feels magical. The air is fresh. It energises you. It rejuvenates you. It helps you see the beauty of being in the moment. You don't crave for a cigarette to start your day. Earlier it might be your habit to look for a cigarette first thing in the morning. But you are no longer a slave of those cigarettes. You are the master of your life. You have made a decision to be a non-smoker and you are sticking to it effortlessly. And you can see the positive changes in your health and wellbeing. You feel so fit and healthy. You have so much energy now. You accomplish all your tasks productively and you don't crave for smoking a cigarette. You no longer feel stressed out. You have realised that having a cigarette to ease stress was an excuse. You have learnt to effectively manage your stress without burning a cigarette – and that feels so great. You are now in complete control of your life. You no longer feel the urge to smoke when experience stress. In fact, you hardly feel stressed nowadays and if there's a thing or two that worries you a bit you have found healthy ways to cope up. You are still enjoying all the good feelings you once associated with cigarette and at the same time you lead a healthy, stress-free life of a non-smoker. You are genuinely happy with your life. Everything seems to be working in your favour. You have taken back the control over your life.

[5 seconds pause]

As a non-smoker now you feel so many positive changes in your life. Your senses have become much sharper than before. Now whenever you sit to eat, you enjoy your food so much more. You take in every bite mindfully fully savouring the textures and flavours of the food. You didn't know food could taste so tasty! Not just that you are now satisfied with less food. You had always wanted to control your diet but now as a non-smoker you eat what you want, you enjoy your food and still maintain your ideal weight and size. Clearly, the benefits of being a non-smoker are much more than you had ever imagined. And you are soaking in all the benefits. You realise that your eyesight has improved. You are not just looking, but seeing. The visuals have become so much crisp and clear. And now you can hear the symphonies of nature. Your sense of hearing has improved although you might not have had any issues with your sense of hearing as a smoker but now since you have become a non-smoker you can notice your hearing becoming sharper and better. And also your sense of smell; you can now notice the fragrance and aroma around you so much well. And the same goes for your sense of touch. It's just magical. The life as a non-smoker has so much hidden benefits. And now you are enjoying them fully. Your life as non-smoker is so much richer and better than before. You engage more. You involve more. And you get the most out of whatever you do. Your improvement and progress is visible to all. You are being appreciated. And not just that you feel so good about yourself. You never knew life could be lived that way. You had always wanted to live a good life but you never imagined it could be this much good. As if the decision to quit smoking was the turning point in your life. Everything that you wanted to have is with you now. You are living a superb family life. Your family appreciate what you do for them. They appreciate your decision to quit smoking and your commitment to keep that promise. They respect you so much more now. And you are so much happy.

[5 seconds pause]

And as a non-smoker, you look at the world from a new level of awareness. You have clarity of thought. You can think so much better. Your memory is so sharp and excellent. You notice the subtle changes that are now making your life so much easier and better. As if you have become so much more sensitive to good things in life. You are meeting new people who are appreciating you for who you are. They are in awe of your personality. And it surely has something to do with you being a non-smoker. You are being acknowledged and recognized at work.

Your talents and skills are shining bright. You are making tremendous progress at work. You are so productive and efficient. And not just work, even outside of work your productivity is growing so fast. You enjoy each moment your day and are more productive than ever. You take out time to do the things you have always wanted to do. You are going to places you have always wanted to visit. And without the baggage of carrying you box of cigarettes. It feels so relaxing and liberating. You are living the life you knew you are meant to live. And all this is happening because of your decision to quit smoking. Life is shining bright. You are so much relaxed and at peace with yourself. Finally you are living the life of your dreams. You are living without regrets or remorse. You are in charge of your life. You dictate your terms. You are the master of your destiny. You no longer crave for that cigarette. Now, when you see someone smoke the same brand that you used to smoke earlier, you feel repulsed. Now you don't crave for that cigarette. You just can't stand the sight of that cigarette because your subconscious mind has been rewired into you giving up all that doesn't serve you. Now the chemicals in your body respond in a different way. And it doesn't mean you are losing any good feelings that you once associated with smoking. You will continue to feel those good feelings but never again will you feel the urge to smoke. And this change has settled in your subconscious mind. This change has settled in your body and your cells. And this change is everlasting. You live this changed life of ideal health and wellbeing. This beautiful inner change is spilling over into your outside world. You now see your life as a gift. You want to be alive, be aware, and be involved in every aspect of life. You see every day as a unique opportunity to give your best. You give each day the importance it deserves. Now, for you, each day is so special. You wake up full of energy and excitement. You do your morning exercise, you do your morning rituals and you begin each day with a bang. There is so much excitement in the air. Each moment is so fresh. Each day, you feel more alive and purposeful than before. As if life has taken a complete one eighty degree turn for you. You do the things you love to do. And whatever you do, you enjoy completely. You are now so much involved in each moment, in each activity. There is joy in everything you do because you do it with so much passion and energy. And you spend your day with full awareness and energy. You are always calm and anchored. When around people, you are graceful and confident. You make others feel comfortable. Not just that, you are comfortable in your own skin. As a non-smoker you manage your day quite effortlessly, completing tasks and taking out time for your hobbies as well. The inner peace you feel is indescribable. You need no reason to be happy. As a non-smoker, you can see a drastic change in how you respond to outside events. You seldom get angry or feel irritated. You don't get stressed. You have made peace with your past and you no longer worry about the future. Your health is at its peak and you are effortlessly maintaining that level of health and fitness.

[5 seconds pause]

You are enjoying all the benefits of being a non-smoker. The positive changes in your health are visible to others as well. Everyone can notice the shine on your skin, the sparkle in your eyes, and the confidence in your demeanor. But you know that the change visible to others on the outside is a byproduct of the positive changes that are happening on the inside. There is a deep cleansing process that is happening in your body. All the deposits of tars and negative influence of smoking are being flushed out from your body. There is no sort of harmful deposits now left in your body. You have been completely cleansed and healed. And you feel so grateful for this transformation. You are healthy from the inside and that shows on the outside. Your entire being is healthy. All your cells, all your organs are healthy and are doing their work perfectly. The energy flows within you perfectly. You feel strong. And you feel strong and energetic all the times. You enjoy the health benefits of a non-smoker. You breathe in fresh air and your lungs feel so good. And you no longer feel the craving to smoke. You always remember of your decision to quit smoking. You always remember that you have come so far in your journey. And if you have come so far, you can always go farther. Your subconscious mind knows how to cope with the stress without making you burn a cigarette. Whenever you feel any stress, your body's inner chemistry will take care of it. You will continue to feel the benefits you associated with smoking but you will never smoke again. You have become a non-smoker. And you are enjoying each moment of this life now – this beautiful, healthy life as a non-smoker. You know that your subconscious mind has been programmed to help you never smoke again. Your body's internal chemistry, your, cells, and organs have adapted to help you continue to lead your life as a non-smoker because you deserve to live a healthy life. You deserve to breathe in the freshness from around you. You deserve peace of mind. You have made a decision to quit smoking. And your subconscious mind has listened to you. It has listened to all the instructions in the hypnosis very sincerely, even if your conscious mind wandered away. Your subconscious mind knows what needs to be done. And it has already sprung into action. It has alerted your cells about their new roles. It will manage the altered chemistry of your body. Your body will be so much relaxed now. As you get up, as you open your eyes, and resume your day, you will notice how much relaxed you feel now. You didn't feel so good at the start of the hypnosis. But now, you feel so good, so relaxed. While you were in this hypnosis, positive changes have happened in your body and will soon manifest in your life.

[5 seconds pause]

Now I will be counting backwards from five to zero. And when I reach zero, I want you to open your eyes, be fully aware of your body and your surroundings.

Five. Become conscious of your existence.

Four. Begin to feel your body. Bring your awareness to different areas of your body. Feel the sensations in your feet and hands. Wiggle your toes and fingers. Rotate your wrists. Feel your arms. Be very gentle. Take your time and feel the connection with your physical body.

Three. Bring your awareness to how you feel. You may notice that you feel so much more relaxed and comfortable than you were in the beginning of this meditation.

Two. You can feel the flow of energy in your body. You feel so much refreshed and full of positive energy. This flow rejuvenates you.

One. You bring your awareness to the present moment. Feel your breath. Focus on the in-breath and the out-breath. The in-breath and the out-breath. The in-breath and the out-breath. Now become aware of your sense of hearing. What do you hear in your surroundings? Is there any noise coming from inside the room or from the outside?

And zero. Gently open your eyes. Be very gentle. Take your time. You may blink your eyes to let them adjust. Now relax. Be fully aware and alert. Welcome back!

5. Quit smoking Hypnosis – V (70 minutes)

Today, I am going to fix your habit of smoking by reprogramming your subconscious mind. Just like a computer is run by software, your body is run by your habits. These habits, whether good or bad decide the course of your life. The good news is that you can change the course of your life by tweaking these habits. And that's what we are going to do today. I am going to reprogramme your subconscious mind by taking you into a hypnotic trance.

Do not listen to this audio if you are doing something that needs your conscious awareness. Preferably lie down on a bed or a comfortable sofa or sit in a relaxed position.

To make you quit smoking I am going to dig deep and work on the very reasons you smoke. So, tell me why do you crave for a cigarette? Is it to release stress or to take a break from your work? And what feelings do you associate with smoking? Is it a feeling of de-stressing, a relaxed mind, or do you experience a certain kind of joy from smoking?

In this hypnosis meditation I am going to command your subconscious mind to find ways to enjoy the same good feelings you get from a cigarette but you will do so without actually smoking one.

These feelings of stress release and relaxation don't come from the cigarette but they are produced within your body. And your body can release the same chemicals even without you smoking a cigarette. So instead of depending on the external stimulus that is harming your health, I will command your subconscious mind to tap into the internal resources. The space of calmness and stress-release lies within you and you are going to tap into that mental space to access the good feelings.

[5 seconds pause]

I want you to place your left hand on your chest-centre and your right hand on your stomach. Feel the breaths – the in-breath and the out-breath. Feel the connection.

Feel your breath coming into your body and leaving your body in its own natural rhythm. Like waves coming in against the sea shore. You can take a moment to notice where your body is making contact with the ground. Whether it's a bed, sofa, or a chair. Just notice what is supporting the weight of your body. Notice the sensation of that contact, so from your back, you notice where your head is touching, your arms, hands, your legs, your feet. And just allow yourself to be really held and be supported in this moment. Focus on being really present for the sensation of body touches the ground with the bed. Just really relax into the weight of your body.

[5 seconds pause]

Breathing in, bring our awareness all the way down to our body, to your right foot and try and sense what life is like for your right foot. Feel from the inside of your foot. You might notice what the skin of your foot can feel. So it might feel a sock, it might be inside your shoes or slipper. Just notice what it makes contact with. Whether it's the heel of your foot or if you have curled up the side of your foot. Just notice what sensations, what external textures and pressure your foot can feel from outside. And then notice how the temperature of the feels for your right foot. Does it feel neutral? Does it feel warm? Or cool? It may be the worn part of the foot. It may be that one part feels warm and another part feels cold. Simply observe what your right foot is feeling. Notice if it feels squeezed or it if feels spacious. And allow the entire foot to be filled with this heavy and relaxed energy. Feeling relaxed; breathe in, breathe out. So let every part of your foot and all your cells to be filled with this really deep and heavy energy of relaxation. So that it can rest very deeply in the present movement as you allow your right foot to let go of everything.

[5 seconds pause]

Now on your next inhale shift your awareness to the left foot. Just take a moment to explore your left foot and see what its experience is, right now. From the heel of your foot moving across the sole and all the way down to your five toes. Just notice, what sensations your foot is feeling right now. What textures, what sensation of pressure from the outside and then what temperature it feels. Is it warm; is it cool? Does it feel spacious? Does it feel squeezed? Just take a moment to explore the experience of your foot right now. Really infuse your entire foot with your heavy relaxed energy; so that your foot totally fills with this energy of relaxation and is able to rest completely. Feeling relaxed; breathe in, breathe out.

[5 seconds pause]

Now bring your awareness to the both your ankles. Just be aware of the ankle joints. If they feel at ease, if there is a feeling of an ache or a tension. And your intention towards your ankles should be to simply allow them to let go of whatever they are holding on to.

Feeling relaxed; breathe in, breathe out. So, offer them this heavy energy and feeling of relaxation. So that they know it's completely fine to relax, it's a good time to really rest. So let both joints be filled with this heavy relaxed energy. They may fall open a little bit by back. This is a result of letting go. This body relaxation practice is a very important part of this hypnosis as it is taking you into deeper and deeper levels of the hypnotic trance. The more your body relaxes, the more ably your subconscious mind receives my command and charts out different ways to act on them. So, continuing with this relaxation.

[5 seconds pause]

Now, I want you to bring your awareness to your calves, to your two calves. Feel as if you yourself are your two calves so that you can understand their experience and actually learn what they feel right now. Your calf muscles hold a lot of tension. So just notice if they have the gripping quality into the muscles. And then offer them this very heavy and relaxed energy. Feeling relaxed; breathe in, breathe out. So let it move upwards to the ankles and filling your two calves. Your calves and your feet run us around so much of the day for you. They work so hard. Now they want to relax. Let them rest quietly. So let this heavy relaxed energy really fill your two calves and let them rest completely.

[5 seconds pause]

This body relaxation practice is a very important part of this hypnosis as it is taking you into deeper and deeper levels of the hypnotic trance. The more your body relaxes, the more ably your subconscious mind receives my command and charts out different ways to act on them. So, continuing with this relaxation now. Bring that heavy relaxed energy up to fill up your left knee. And you really want to have every aspect of the joints to be saturated with this heavy relaxed energy. So your balls and sockets, muscular shins around, the skin that surrounds, the blood that moves through the joints. You want to breathe in that energy with the way that the joints can feel, that it's safe to relax. Feeling relaxed; breathe in, breathe out.

[5 seconds pause]

 Bring that heavy relaxed energy up to fill up your right knee. And you really want to have every aspect of the joints to be saturated with this heavy relaxed energy. So your balls and sockets, muscular shins around, the skin that surrounds, the blood that moves through the joints. You want to breathe in that energy with the way that the joints can feel, that it's safe to relax. Feeling relaxed; breathe in, breathe out.

[5 seconds pause]

Now move your awareness to your left thigh. Let this heavy relaxed energy begin to fill your left thigh. We have large muscles here; they do a lot of work for us. Just see as that heavy relaxed energy spreads through your thigh. If it's possible for your muscles to let go some tension, to really rest fully and let themselves be really supported. Feeling relaxed; breathe in, breathe out.

[5 seconds pause]

Now move your awareness to your right thigh. Let this heavy relaxed energy begin to fill your right thigh. We have large muscles here; they do a lot of work for us. Just see as that heavy relaxed energy spreads through your thigh, if it's possible for your muscles to let go some tension. To really rest fully and let themselves be really supported. Feeling relaxed; breathe in, breathe out.

[5 seconds pause]

Now shift your awareness to your pelvis, the creedal of your hips, your lower back, your hips, your lower belly. Just breathe into this area. And let it begin to fill with heavy relaxed energy. Feeling relaxed; breathe in, breathe out; so that its weight can truly rest.

[5 seconds pause]

From the base of our spine you can trace the line of the spine. Slowly up your back. You allow this heavy relaxed energy to fill up your spine. Feeling relaxed; breathe in, breathe out.

[5 seconds pause]

Feel it moving up to your lower spine to your middle, to your upper spine area. And then expand your awareness outward from your spine; you take in the muscles of your lower back so that bands of muscles that come back, your ribcage, your shoulder blades. So that the whole landscape of your back is clear in your awareness. And it fills with heavy relaxed energy and rest fully and completely. Feeling relaxed; breathe in, breathe out.

[5 seconds pause]

Feel each vertebrae getting relaxed. Feeling relaxed; breathe in, breathe out. Our life is so much richer for having a healthy spine. It gives stability and balance. Now, you have an opportunity to allow all relax and reenergize your spinal column. Feeling relaxed; breathe in, breathe out.

[5 seconds pause]

Now, I want you to shift your focus to the top of your shoulders. Just notice how they are feeling right now. You might imagine someone places hand on your shoulder; a reassuring touch to let them know that it's completely fine to relax. It's completely fine to let go. So let the two shoulders fill with this heavy relaxed energy. Feeling relaxed; breathe in, breathe out. And if you notice pockets of tension or resistance to relax, you can visualize the release of that tension as vapors being released out of your body giving a sense of ease in that area. Feeling relaxed; breathe in, breathe out.

[5 seconds pause]

Relaxation is very important. You know how much your body and mind need this relaxation. So whenever your mind wanders away, bring it back to my voice and continue to enjoy this relaxation practice.

So let's move on. From the top of your shoulders you move down to your left arm and let it be filled with this heavy relaxed energy. Upper arm filling relaxing, your elbow joints, breathing a sense of ease into the joint. And letting it rest and relax. And your left forearm, letting them be totally at rest. Filling with the heavy energy of relaxation. Feeling relaxed; breathe in, breathe out.

[5 seconds pause]

Then coming into the fine bones of wrist. Breathing in such a way that you offer a sense of spaciousness, relaxation to the details joints of our wrists. Feeling relaxed; breathe in, breathe out. Then you come in to embody your left hand fully. Resting in your left hand and residing within its presence can be a very peaceful place to be in. Feeling relaxed; breathe in, breathe out.

[5 seconds pause]

Now, I want you to repeat the same process for your right arm and let it be filled with this heavy relaxed energy. Upper arm filling relaxing, your elbow joints, breathing a sense of ease into the joint. And letting it rest and relax. And your right forearm, letting them be totally at rest. Filling with the heavy energy of relaxation. Then coming into the fine bones of wrist. Feeling relaxed; breathe in, breathe out.

[5 seconds pause]

Breathing in such a way that you offer a sense of spaciousness, relaxation to the details joints of our wrists. Then you come in to embody your right hand fully. Resting in your right hand and residing within its presence can be a very peaceful place to be in. Feeling relaxed; breathe in, breathe out.

[5 seconds pause]

This body relaxation practice is a very important part of this hypnosis as it is taking you into deeper and deeper levels of the hypnotic trance. The more your body relaxes, the more ably your subconscious mind receives my command and charts out different ways to act on them. So, continuing with this relaxation now. Then bringing your attention back to your lower belly, to your lower abdomen; just breathing deeply into that space. Feeling relaxed; breathe in, breathe out; offering space to our internal organs. They have such wisdom. Our lower intestine knows what nutrients to retain, what our body needs and they work hard. So we let them fill with this heavy relaxed energy now, really rest in this space. Feeling relaxed; breathe in, breathe out. They might feel nourished, restored. Then inviting that energy to move upwards to our upper abdomen or stomach or liver or pancreas you let all our internal organs be bathed in this heavy relaxed energy; so that they can really rest; so That they can heal. They work so hard for us. Feeling relaxed; breathe in, breathe out.

[5 seconds pause]

This body relaxation practice is a very important part of this hypnosis as it is taking you into deeper and deeper levels of the hypnotic trance. The more your body relaxes, the more ably your subconscious mind receives my command and charts out different ways to act on them. So, continuing with this relaxation now.

Now, shift your awareness to your chest area. You bring your awareness to rising and falling of your lungs. They have taken so many breaths for you. They have been working tirelessly to keep you healthy and alive. Let them fill with this heavy relaxed energy. Feeling relaxed; breathe in, breathe out.

[5 seconds pause]

Bring your awareness to your heart. You may be able to feel its beating rhythm. Or sense of pulse of blood moving through your body. Feel your heart beat. Your heart has been beating for you since you have breathed air. Even when you rest at night and sleep our heart keeps working for us and you have this opportunity now to offer gratitude or kindness to our heart and let it really rest in this heavy relaxed energy. Its beating is very gentle and steady. All the tissues around the heart can feel heavy relaxed energy with the heart beating steadily in its rhythm. Feeling relaxed; breathe in, breathe out.

[5 seconds pause]

Now bring your awareness to the very upper part of your chest. See how it feels. Is it at ease? Allow this relaxed energy to saturate this region and reach up to the right part of your shoulders. Draw this energy up to your neck. Let that heavy relaxed energy begin to fill that area. Feeling relaxed; breathe in, breathe out.

[5 seconds pause]

Now feel it moving into your throat and the very upper part of your spine. Our Neck can hold a lot of tension very easily. If you are lying down the neck has no work to do at the movement, does not need to hold up our head and really rest deeply. So breathe in such a way that this energy of relaxation and ease all the way of our neck; offering it a way of relaxation, of deep relaxation, of healing. Feeling relaxed; breathe in, breathe out.

[5 seconds pause]

Draw your awareness up your skull and around whole way down your face. Notice the weight of your scalp against the ground. Just notice that heaviness of your head, of your face. Just let it rest very deeply. Feeling relaxed; breathe in, breathe out. You can let our brain rest totally inside your skull; just let it be held by your skeleton. Feeling relaxed; breathe in, breathe out.

[5 seconds pause]

Then bring your awareness to your forehead; trying to feel your forehead from inside. And let it fill with this heavy relaxed energy across your forehead. As if someone resting there hand on it for moment to reassure you that it is ok to let go, it's completely fine to relax.

[5 seconds pause]

Now bring your awareness to your eyes; your eyeballs resting inside the eye sockets. Feeling relaxed; breathe in, breathe out. See if they can feel a little bit heavier as they fill with this energy of relaxation as it suffuses the area around your eyes, your eyebrows, and the skin around your eyes. Your eyelids the inside of your eyelids, let them all filled with this energy of relaxation with this intention to let go, to rest really deeply. Feeling relaxed; breathe in, breathe out.

[5 seconds pause]

All the colors that we can see, a friends face smiling, member of our family laughing, such beauty we have seen in nature, in human beings, sunsets, skies, all the colors, all the beauties which literally takes our breaths away. We have all this richness because of our two eyes. So send gratitude to every cell in our two eyes and thank them.

[5 seconds pause]

Now bring your awareness to your nose. You try to feel our nose to sense it from inside. Fill it with heavy relaxed energy. They know it's completely fine to rest. Feeling relaxed; breathe in, breathe out. You have smelled such beautiful things because of your working nose, because of your healthy nose. Flowers in a garden, pine trees, or smell after the rain, lilies, sweet pie, jasmine, and such beauties. You enjoy your food so much more because of your healthy nose. You smell the fresh air or moist soil – so many riches because of your healthy nose. Feeling relaxed; breathe in, breathe out.

[5 seconds pause]

Relaxation is very important. You know how much your body and mind need this relaxation. So whenever your mind wanders away, bring it back to my voice and continue to enjoy this relaxation practice. Breathing in, you bring your awareness to your two ears. You try an experience your ears from the inside. From the very depth of the ear cannel you fill with the heavy relaxed energy; filling your ear lobes, filling your whole ear; knowing that it's completely fine to relax. Feeling relaxed; breathe in, breathe out. You don't need to be alert to anything. They have no job at the moment. What sense have you heard in your lives? The sense which has given such happiness, or inspiration or support, the assurance, sense of your dearest friends, sense of laughter, sense of music which fill your heart, they bring energy; and listening to the music of birds' melodious songs and so many things.

[5 seconds pause]

Bring your awareness to your jaw. So you become aware of your jaw and the bone or the muscles. You allow it to fill with this heavy relaxed energy; so that your entire jaw, muscles stretching up behind your ears. Everything knows that its completely fine to rest, it's completely fine to relax. Feeling relaxed; breathe in, breathe out. You let your jaw rest. Feeling relaxed; breathe in, breathe out.

[5 seconds pause]

You bring your awareness to your lips. You let your lips rest. You fill this heavy relaxed energy then inside your mouth you become aware of your gums or teeth or tongue you let them all rest really deeply.

[5 seconds pause]

You notice the roof of your tongue, very base of your tongue, where you can sometime hold tensions. And you offer that this opportunity to feel completely at ease to rest.

[5 seconds pause]

Now bring your awareness from the crown of your head all the way down to your body. Through your head and neck, throat all the way down to your back, torso, and your arms, your hips, flow of your hips to your two legs, all the way down, down till you feel your ten toes. You scan for moment and see if there is any area that might let go of more tension, might offer even more weight to the bed or to the ground. So that you could be held even more in this moment, supported even more.

[5 seconds pause]

Surrender in the beauty of this moment. Let go of any thoughts that have been troubling you lately. This moment is for relaxation. Feel the gentle rhythm of your breathing. Feel the beating of your heart. And bring your awareness on the flow of your breath – the in-breath and the out-breath.

[3 minutes pause]

You might have missed a part of this hypnosis. It doesn't matter. Your subconscious mind was busy listening to my commands and it has already sprung into action looking for ways to turn you into a non-smoker.

[30 seconds pause]

Your subconscious mind will find ways to get rid of the unhealthy habits and effects of smoking. It knows how to best achieve this goals without missing out on the good feelings you get from smoking. Your subconscious mind will work in a way so that you enjoy the best of both the worlds – the good feelings you get from smoking and health benefits of a non-smoker. Now you will never again smoke a cigarette in life. This change will happen and yet you will continue to keep the good feeling you get from smoking. You will be a non-smoker for the rest of your life and yet keep with you all the good things you enjoyed because of your old habits. Your body will automatically adjust to help you manage your feelings and emotions. You will no longer be a slave to cigarettes. From now on, you will be the ones taking the shots. You will be in complete control of yourself. And you won't have to do any extra efforts for that because your subconscious mind knows how to make adjustments to keep the good effects of old habits. So rest deeply because your subconscious mind is being reprogrammed to change your habits and turn you into a non-smoker once and for all.

[5 seconds pause]

You know how healthy it is to be a non-smoker. Think about the very reasons you wish to quit smoking. Think about how good you will feel as a non-smoker. You will see a pack of your favourite brand of cigarettes and yet feel no craving or compulsion to smoke. Your health will be at its ideal best. Your lungs can breathe in the fresh air. Your decision to quit smoking is doing wonders for your physical and mental health. You are so much confident now. You are so much in control of your emotions. You manage your life so effortlessly. On work front you are now at your productive best. And it has all to do with your decision to quit smoking once and for all.

[5 seconds pause]

There is a deep cleansing process that is happening in your physical body. For long you had been ignoring your health and wellbeing. But since you have quit smoking, you can see the positive transformation happen deep within your body. All the deposits of tars, residues and negative influence of smoking are being flushed out from your body. A sort of catharsis is happening deep within you.

[5 seconds pause]

Now, you are free of all the negativities. There is no sort of harmful deposits now left in your body. You have been completely cleansed and healed. And you feel so grateful for this transformation. You are healthy from the inside and that shows on the outside. Your entire being is healthy. All your cells, all your organs are healthy and are doing their work perfectly. The energy flows within you perfectly. You feel strong. And you feel strong and energetic all the times. You enjoy the health benefits of a non-smoker.

[5 seconds pause]

And all this started with your commitment to become a non-smoker and remain one for the rest of your life. The journey has been fruitful for you. You are now in complete control of your life. You no longer feel the urge to smoke when experience stress. In fact, you hardly feel stressed nowadays and if there's a thing or two that worries you a bit you have found healthy ways to cope up. You are still enjoying all the good feelings you once associated with cigarette and at the same time you lead a healthy, stress-free life of a non-smoker. And you are enjoying every moment of this new life. You feel so much grateful. It feels great to have control back in your hands. And it feels almost magical. You, the non-smoker you of the future now looks back at the smoker you of the past. What advice would you give to yourself?

[5 seconds pause]

Think about it. How did you manage to pull it off? Take your time. Do not try too hard because the question is really for your subconscious mind to let it find ways to achieve the goals to help you become a non-smoker. And it is already in action. No doubt smoking a cigarette gave you some benefits like stress-relief. But all those benefits were temporary. Your subconscious mind has been rewired to make you enjoy the same benefits you enjoyed from smoking without lighting a cigarette again. And it's all possible. And it's all happening. You just relax. Simply let go of all the doubts and worries. Let the change happen organically. For then the change will be everlasting and effective.

[10 minutes pause]

You can bring your awareness to the movement of your breath. Notice how relaxed your breathing has become now. Notice how rhythmic it is now. It has now become so gentle and smooth. You may notice that your body is now much more relaxed and at peace than at the beginning. You may stay in this relaxed state for a while.

[2 minutes pause]

Now, as I count backwards from five to zero, I want you to bring your awareness back to the present, back to your body, and back to your consciousness.

Five. Bring your consciousness back to your body. Slowly begin to realise that you are in your physical body. Coming back to the awareness.

Four. Feel your body. Feel your feet, your legs, and your hips. Feel your abdomen and your chest region. Feel your entire spinal column, feel your back. Be aware of your hands and wrists and your elbows and your entire arms. Now your shoulders and neck and chin. Now bring your awareness into your entire face. Feel your eyes resting in your sockets; now your forehead and your scalp. In a moment, be aware of your entire physical body.

Three. Clench your fists. And release. Move your fingers and toes. Loosen up your shoulders. Rotate your ankles, knees. Relax your jaw.

Two. Feel the flow of energy. Be in the present moment. Feel your breath. Feel the sensations.

One. Be aware of the surroundings. Can you hear any sound coming from outside the room? Can you smell anything? Begin to blink your eyes.

Zero. When you are ready, gently open your eyes, and return to the physical world.

www.ingramcontent.com/pod-product-compliance
Lightning Source LLC
Chambersburg PA
CBHW072152100526
44589CB00015B/2196